# COMPASSION
### AND
# MEDITATION

# COMPASSION
## AND
# MEDITATION

### THE SPIRITUAL DYNAMIC BETWEEN
### BUDDHISM AND CHRISTIANITY

JEAN-YVES LELOUP

Translated by Joseph Rowe

Inner Traditions

Rochester, Vermont • Toronto, Canada

Inner Traditions
One Park Street
Rochester, Vermont 05767
www.InnerTraditions.com

Copyright © 2000, 2007 by Éditions Albin Michel S. A.
English translation © 2009 by Inner Traditions International

Originally published in French under the title *La Montagne dans L'Océan* by
Albin Michel, Paris
First U.S. edition published in 2009 by Inner Traditions

**Library of Congress Cataloging-in-Publication Data**

Leloup, Jean-Yves.
  [Montagne dans l'océan. English]
  Compassion and meditation : the spiritual dynamic between Buddhism and
Christianity / Jean-Yves Leloup ; translated by Joseph Rowe.—1st U.S. ed.
      p. cm.
  Includes index.
  ISBN 978-1-59477-277-1 (pbk.)
  1. Christianity and other religions—Buddhism. 2. Buddhism—Relations—
Christianity. 3. Compassion. 4. Meditation. 5. Buddhism—Doctrines. I. Title.
  BR128.B8L4513 2006
  261.2'43—dc22

                                                                    2009010572

Printed and bound in the United States by Lake Book Manufacturing

10  9  8  7  6  5  4  3  2  1

Text design and layout by Priscilla Baker
This book was typeset in Garamond Premier Pro with Granjon and Gill Sans used
as display typefaces

Inner Traditions wishes to express its appreciation for assistance given by the
government of France through the National Book Office of the Ministère de la
Culture in the preparation of this translation.

Nous tenons à exprimer nos plus vifs remerciements au government de la France
et le ministère de la Culture, Centre National du Livre, pour leur concours dans le
préparation de la traduction de cet ouvrage.

*To Father Seraphim*

*To Mount Athos*

*To the Dalai Lama, Ocean of Compassion*

# CONTENTS

# INTRODUCTION

There are questions that cannot be answered by reading books or listening to lectures—unless they lead us into practices or exercises—which exhaust the question, allowing the answer to spring forth from the very secret of our being and our breath . . .

Even more valuable are encounters with individuals who use various skillful means to undermine our own most clever responses. They introduce us to a path, which demands of us that we verify for ourselves, day-by-day, moment-by-moment, that the Real is indeed present in our experience. Then we see that the source of our deepest suffering is our habit of always being somewhere else.

After many wanderings and blind alleys, I had the good fortune to encounter such people and their teachings. I have recounted this in my earlier book in French, *L'Absurde et la Grâce* (Absurdity and Grace).

Today, the question I am most often asked is this: in our contemporary world, what kind of practice is most essential and most capable of helping us to make sense of this world? My reply is unhesitating: the marriage of meditation and compassion. Without compassion, meditation tends to become a form of self-hypnosis, a subtle form of narcissism and escapism. And without meditation, compassion tends to degenerate into an activism with good intentions but lacking in depth and discrimination.

When I point this out, people often respond with the cliché that the practice of meditation belongs to Buddhism, and the practice of compassion belongs to Christianity—as if silence or love could be considered a kind of "territory" belonging to one religion or another! In this view, the practice of meditation together with compassion is reduced to a kind of syncretism: "Buddhism combined with Christianity."

One of the first fruits of the regular practice of meditation and compassion is freedom from undue concern regarding the reductionist opinions and judgments of others. Nevertheless, we must insist that Christianity is also a tradition of meditation, and that Buddhism is an ancient practice of compassion.

I wish to thank the Philosophy Religion International Network for their work in the transcriptions of the cassettes of some of my lectures, which have been used in this book: at the Dojo Zen in Paris, on meditation; and those given at the Franciscan convent, Chant de l'Oiseau, in Brussels.

Thus in Buddhist contexts, I have spoken of Christianity, and in Christian contexts, of Buddhism. In doing this, my ground has always been the teachings and practices I have learned from those who have guided me in these two traditions. Therefore, I wish to express once more my gratitude and appreciation to these teachers. We can only transmit what we have received . . . never forgetting that what we have been able to receive is far less than the totality of what we have been offered.

The transcribers have deliberately preserved the informal style of oral communication and have avoided weighing down the text with the scriptural references that would have been appropriate in a more scholarly work. The goal of this work is to invite the reader toward a life of more silence and more love, inhabited by that wisdom and compassion, which are not the province of any particular religion but the ground of being of all humans, whatever their doubts or beliefs.

It is in this spirit that I have also been happy to participate in the conferences and pilgrimages of the OTU (Organisation des traditions unies),[1] in desert surroundings, at Bodhgaya in India, and on the shores of Lake Tiberiade in Israel. As the Archbishop Anastasios, Primate of the Orthodox Church of Albania, once said: "More time and more means must be found to bring about true and spontaneous meetings so as to generate Friendship . . ."

The Dalai Lama has also said: "From my own experience, I have learned that the most effective method for overcoming conflict is close contact and exchange between people of different beliefs—not only on an intellectual level, but also through deep spiritual experiences. This is a powerful means of developing mutual understanding and respect. It is through such exchange that a solid foundation can be established to bring about true harmony."*

Before we celebrate this understanding between our different sages, honesty compels us to briefly recall some of the quarrels and confusions of our different scribes. The history of relations between Christianity and Buddhism is of interest here, and we do not have to go very far back in time in order to find the most sectarian invective, as well as the most simplistic syncretism.

In 1735, J. B. du Halde, in his *Description of the Empire of China,* wrote of Buddhism as "an abominable cult." P. Parennin, in his letter to M. de Mairan, went further: "It is a plague and a gangrene. Chinese philosophers were right to combat it, not only as an absurd doctrine, but as a moral monster, which overturns civil society."

To Christians who claim that everything of value in the teaching of the Buddha was taken from the Law of Moses, Buddhists retort that, on the contrary, it was Jews and Christians who plagiarized Buddhist scriptures.

According to an anonymous work from 1881, revealingly entitled *Jesus-Buddha,* both the Essenes and the prophets of Israel are "obviously" Buddhists: the first prophetic schools were Buddhist monasteries.

---

*[Since we were unable to locate the original quotation by the Dalai Lama, which was probably in English, this (along with subsequent quotations by him) is a retro-translation. —*Trans.*]

This Buddhism was altered by Esdras, but soon the Essenes restored the pure doctrine, in which they exalted Jesus in their monastery, rescuing him from ostracism. In this view, it was understandable that Jesus was opposed by the Pharisees as a "bastard product of the ancient Law of Moses and the new Law of Buddha." Having preached this syncretism, Jesus became a Buddha after his death, exalted by his disciples. Another way of stating it is that "Buddha became Jesus" for Westerners.

What these different points of view all have in common is an air of dogmatic self-assurance whose degree of certainty is in direct proportion to the absence of any foundation for their claims. There are those who would reject both the polemics and the facile syncretism of these writings in favor of a subtler syncretism that is full of good intentions, yet, which remains a caricature of both religions. In *The Perfect Way,* another anonymous work from 1882, we find the following:

> Buddha and Jesus are both necessary to each other. Thus in the complete system, Buddha is the intellect, Jesus is the heart; Buddha is the general, Jesus is the particular; Buddha is the brotherhood of the universe, Jesus is the brotherhood of man; Buddha is philosophy, Jesus is religion; Buddha is the circumference, Jesus is the center; Buddha is the system, Jesus is the point of radiance; Buddha is manifestation, Jesus is spirit. In sum, Buddha is man, or intelligence, and Jesus is woman, or intuition. . . . No one can be a true Christian unless he is first of all a Buddhist. Thus the two religions constitute, respectively, the exterior and the interior of the same Gospel. Buddhism is its foundation (for it includes Pythagoreanism), and Christianity is its illumination. Just as Buddhism is incomplete without Christianity, so Christianity is incomprehensible without Buddhism.

One would suppose that the twentieth century, with its deeper knowledge of the founding texts of both civilizations, would be less prone to indulge in assertive judgments regarding the "other."

This is unfortunately not the case with Paul Claudel:*

For a human being to whom God has shown and offered himself, it is all too true that the temptation of Buddhism is to choose the silence of a creature withdrawn into a total refusal, into the incestuous tranquility of a soul anchored in its essential singularity. Man carries within him a natural refusal of any spirituality that falls short of the Absolute, and the desire to free himself from the dreadful circle of vanity. But if he thinks he can succeed in this endeavor by following in the footsteps of [the Buddha]—no doubt the most profound of those spiritual beings left to the sole resources of their own lights—he denies the faith he has received from above. In this, he will only succeed in "perfecting the pagan blasphemy." This apostasy is also a form of mental regression.[2]

Let us also quote two famous twentieth-century theologians, beginning with Henri de Lubac:

Human religions and wisdom traditions are not like diverse paths winding in different ways up toward the peak of a unique mountain. A better comparison of their different ideals would be that of separate mountain peaks, with chasms between them. The pilgrim who has strayed from the only true direction leading to the highest of these summits risks ultimately finding himself even further from that summit. Finally, it is between these high peaks that the flash of the greatest conflicts breaks forth.[3]

And Romano Guardini:

The Buddha is a great mystery. He lives in a frightening, almost

---

*[Paul Claudel (1868–1955) was a famous French essayist, poet, dramatist, and diplomat. In his youth, he abandoned scientific materialism and converted to a conservative form of Catholicism. —*Trans.*]

superhuman freedom; yet he is also a powerful source of goodness, like a cosmic force. Perhaps Buddha is the ultimate religious genius with which Christianity will have to deal. No one has yet elucidated the Christian significance of the Buddha. Perhaps the Christ not only has precursors in the Old Testament and in John the Baptist, last of the prophets, but also two others: one in the heart of ancient civilization, namely Socrates; and another whose teaching is the summation of Oriental philosophy and religious asceticism: namely, Buddha.[4]

These theological quotations are significant, because they lucidly articulate thoughts that many Catholics and Protestants still harbor today. This being said, we must not underestimate the great change of attitude in many contemporary Christians who refuse to content themselves with reading secondhand opinions about Eastern traditions, but dare to encounter "the others" directly, and experience their spiritual practices. This category includes Christians such as Enomiya Lassalle, A. M. Besnard, Kakichi Dadawaki, Pierre-François de Béthune, as well as their precursors: Thomas Merton, R. Pannikar, Karl Graf von Durkheim, W. Johnston, Father Bede Griffiths, and others.

Perhaps we should henceforth set aside the use of "Christian" or "Buddhist" labels, in favor of entering more deeply into the question: *What is a human being?* What is this profundity that goes by so many different names, yet whose highest yearning is to experience being fully human, and thereby become transformed, liberated from fantasy and illusion, and more present with *what is?*

At the end of a Zen sitting, a Buddhist friend had just explained to me that for him the essential things that he had learned from Zen meditation practice were: non-attachment; the unreality of the subject (*anatma*); emptiness (*shunyata*); and attention to the present, without goal or profit. He asked me four questions:

1. Is it possible for a Christian to be without attachment, with-

out desire, without dependency, even with regard to God and Christ?

2. Can a Christian accept the nonreality of the subject?
3. Can a Christian integrate the experience of ultimate reality as emptiness?
4. Can a Christian live with discontinuity, moment by moment, without memory and without plan?

My response was to invite my friend to come for a week of practice in Hesychast meditation in an Orthodox monastery. But I first explained to him that for me, the most important elements of the Hesychast teachings are: inner freedom; giving of oneself (which is the same as self-renunciation); the sense of mystery; not worrying about tomorrow; and not being preoccupied with the past. And I had these four questions for him:

1. Can a Buddhist be free of all attachment and desire, even with regard to the Dharma and the Buddha?
2. Can a Buddhist accept the relative reality of the human subject and relinquish his attachment to beliefs about what is ultimately self or nonself?
3. Can a Buddhist integrate the experience of the ultimate reality as Fullness (*pleroma*), and as Mystery (or "supraluminous darkness," as Dionysius the Theologian would say)?
4. Can a Buddhist live both in the present moment and in history without losing openness to the Eternal (i.e., nontemporal)?

Sometimes the best answer to a question is another question. Is it not by asking questions that we stimulate each other to reach more deeply into our own source and, thereby, approach the Source, both together and in our different ways?

# Part One

# THE WAY
# OF MEDITATION

# ONE

# ZEN AND HESYCHASM

I have been invited to a conference that is taking place in a Zen dojo, a place where men and women come together to practice meditation. The setting is simple, without being austere. We are all sitting in proper meditation posture, and the faces are serious, but relaxed . . .

I have been asked to speak about the Hesychast practice of meditation in Christianity. I will be discussing its origin, its transmission from the early centuries of the Christian era to our time, and will offer a description of the practice itself. I would also like to deal with the question as to whether it has an aim, and what its fruits might be.

I do not take this as an invitation to simply give a lecture, but to share my experience and bear witness to the tradition in which my experience is framed.

We are not here to compare Buddhism with Christianity. It is not our aim to weigh the life, philosophy, and wisdom of Siddhartha Gautama Shakyamuni, known as the Buddha, against that of Yeshua ben Yoseif of Nazareth, known as the Christ. Neither are we here to compare our methods of meditation and discuss their advantages and disadvantages from our different points of view.

Our real purpose is to meditate together: to sit, breathe deeply, and to be quiet both outwardly and (if possible) inwardly. If the Spirit that inhabits us is not a tormented spirit, then in a few hours we may find ourselves the better for it. An indescribable loving-kindness is thus embodied in the world, and we can return to it—not only from a desire for our own well-being but also in a desire to incarnate something of this well-being for others.

Clearly, meditation and compassion are not separate. What you call the Bodhisattva ideal is also the ideal of every Christian. But instead of speaking of ideals, let us speak of the realization to which every human being is called: the actualization of their true being. In this meditation and practice it is important for us to become, not just better Buddhists or better Christians, but more authentic human beings. There are many greedy and clever human animals in this world, but few human beings. Authentic human beings are so rare that I would even go so far as to say that we do not live in a truly human world.

I am not here with you today in the hope that you will become a Christian, nor that I will become a Buddhist. We are here in order to become more human, more awake, more loving. The only use of theory is to clarify and stimulate our practice, to restore its place within the traditions we cherish, and establish a dialogue between us, with resonance that fertilizes our becoming, and that of the world in which we live.

# TWO

# TRANSMISSION

In Christianity, as in Buddhism or Sufism, the goal of meditation is to purify our hearts and minds, so that we become receptacles, or spotless mirrors, for pure light.

When human beings are able to welcome this clear light, which is the radiance and the presence of uncreated Being, it instills in them a state of peace, which is independent of circumstances (health, moods, environment, and so on). In other words, a state of peace that is not merely of the psyche but spiritual or ontological, as well. It is the experience of this reality that early Christians called *hesychia,* the origin of Hesychasm. It is the quest and embrace of a silence and peace that is not of this world. Yet we can feel premonitions of it. And far more importantly, we can live it.

Such an experience is the fruit of oral transmission, from heart to heart, from being to being. This is why Christians, Buddhists, and Sufis attach such importance to belonging to an authentic lineage, which transmits, without corruption, true *praxis,* or practice, and authentic *gnosis,* or contemplation.

In Christianity, we can distinguish two kinds of lineage:

- Historical lineage that is traced back to the apostles who founded the first Churches and communities. James is the founder of the

Church of Jerusalem, John the founder of the Church of Ephesus, Thomas of the Church of India, and so forth—including of course Paul and Peter, founders of the Churches of Antioch and of Rome. "Apostolic succession" is considered to be the seal of authenticity and continuity.

• Alongside the historical lineage (important for institutional Churches) is another, more discreet lineage. It is less encumbered by the duty to define doctrines and rules of conduct for the good of communities, and more concerned with nurturing the practice of a form of prayer or meditation, which has the possibility of bringing about an awakening in each individual. This involves a quality of relation of intimacy with God. It was this relationship that Christ alluded to when he spoke of his Father: the Source, the uncreated Origin of all that lives, thinks, loves, and breathes.

Just as Zen monks formally swear their oaths by the genealogy of masters through which the practice has been transmitted to them, so in Hesychasm one invokes the lineage of the Holy Fathers through whom the true teaching has come—a teaching, which individuals must discover, live, and incarnate for themselves.

## THE SAMARITAN WOMAN

When the disciples asked Jesus: "Rabbi, teach us to pray," he transmitted to them the essence of Jewish prayer, now known as "The Lord's Prayer." Each of its verses is derived from Jewish tradition, in a distilled synthesis of the hopes and longings of the people of Israel, and of all the sages and prophets who preceded Jesus. It is a prayer "for the people," which can be recited in the synagogue or in meetings—a prayer to be recited aloud and in public.

Nevertheless, it can also be recited "in secret" behind closed doors: "For the Father who dwells in secret knows what you need." In Zen tradition this might correspond to the reading or chanting of sutras before entering into silent meditation.

The Lord's Prayer became the official prayer of Christianity, for it was Jesus's own prayer. It reveals to us his longing, and what is good and proper for us to ask for. In the form of liturgy it has been transmitted to us from apostolic times.

Along with this rabbinic prayer, transmitted for the most part to men, there is another prayer, which was transmitted to a woman. She was a Samaritan—which is to say that she belonged to a tribe considered as religious heretics by Jesus's own tribe and religion. When she asked him: "How should we pray? On this mountain, or in Jerusalem?" Jesus answered, "Neither on this mountain nor in Jerusalem . . . It is in spirit and in truth that true worshippers should pray."

The literal translation of the Greek *en pneumatic kais aletheia* makes this much clearer: "It is in the breath (*pneuma* in Greek, *ruakh* in Hebrew, *spiritus* in Latin) and in wakefulness (*a-letheia,* meaning not-forgetting; etymologically from *lethe,* i.e., not being asleep) that they must pray."

*Aletheia* is usually translated as "truth," but might be better translated as "awakening." Hence Jesus never claimed to *possess* the truth, but to *be* the truth. Literally, this means "I am in nonforgetfulness," (*ego eimi aletheia*); in other words, "I am awake." This is strikingly similar to the etymology of "Buddha" from *bodhi:* someone whose mind is awakened. Likewise, the Buddha never claimed to *possess* awakening, but to *be* awake. Once again, we are reminded that awakening, or enlightenment, is not the property of Buddhism, any more than Truth is the property of Christianity. Neither the Buddha nor the Christ belongs exclusively to the communities that were founded in their names. They belong to all people of goodwill, all who are attentive to the secret, which lives in the depths of their breath and their consciousness.

Yeshua reminded the Samaritan woman that prayer is not dependent on any sacred place, whether in Jerusalem or on Mt. Horeb (the sacred mountain of the Samaritans). Thus he led her back to her own heart, the dwelling-place of I AM. Even more than an ontology, Christianity is an *odology* (from *odos,* path), a path, which not only leads outwardly, with rituals and righteous actions, but also inwardly, "where the rivers of the living waters flow"—where the tides of life and breath both support us and carry us beyond.

We noted that this practice was given by Yeshua to a woman, but it would be truer to say that it was addressed to "the Feminine," i.e., to the contemplative dimension that lives in all men and women. In this most intimate dimension of our being, he offers the invitation to pray "in breath and in wakefulness." In contrast, the Lord's Prayer is addressed to the more masculine dimension of human beings in their public and active aspect.

This can help us to understand why Clement of Alexandria and St. Johannes Cassianus alluded to the practice of a secret tradition. They were not referring to some "esoteric" doctrine in the usual sense of that word, but to an awakening of the inner human being (*eso-anthropon*). St. Paul, the Desert Fathers (and much later, Meister Eckhart) also spoke of this secret. The practice itself is simple and natural. In bringing our attention to the breath and in being alert to the present moment, we can be led into the Presence, which is the source of our being and of our love. We are led to the living Image of God in us. This is what is meant by the Christ in me, which is deeper than the personal me.

This practice was developed further, with special postures and the invocation of the sacred Name, synchronized with the rhythm of breathing. But the essential, heart-to-heart transmission began when Yeshua spoke to the Samaritan woman. (In Zen tradition, this direct kind of heart-transmission is known as *I shin den shin.*) From her it was transmitted to St. John, who is the only apostle to speak of her in the canonical gospels. He then transmitted it to St. Mark, the first "Pope" of Egypt (whose contemporary successor is Shenouda III, Coptic Patriarch of Alexandria and Cairo). St. Mark also transmitted this practice to all the elders of Egypt. The list of those whose names we still know begins with Anthony and Paul; these hermits and anchorites then transmitted the practice to monks of different nations. From then on, the practice developed into a tradition called Hesychasm. It flourished especially on Mount Athos, that high holy place of Orthodox Christian spirituality.

It was there that a monk named Seraphim transmitted the tradition to me. He was that type of eccentric known in Russian tradition as "mad in Christ" and often barked loudly. He had been a disciple of the revered Staretz Silouan, whose saintliness has become known in the West through the works of Father Sophrony. Father Seraphim lived near the monastery of St. Pantelimon. During a voyage to England, where he was teaching the prayer of the heart, he spoke to me of the importance of the word of Christ, according to his Staretz: "Keep your mind in hell, but never despair."

"Do not fear the darkest depths of the shadow," he told me, "neither your own personal shadow, nor the collective shadow, nor even the cosmic shadow. But you must not go into those depths alone. Let the Christ and his Spirit accompany you. For he is the light, which no darkness can reach nor quench, the light spoken of in the prologue to the Book of St. John. Each of us carries a mouthful of light into our own night [this is an allusion to the story of Judas, who goes off into the night after having received a mouthful of bread from the hands of Christ], and this spark can never grow dim. It is by dwelling in it that we never despair of ourselves or of the world. This is called 'having no support, but being supported.'"

His teacher, St. Silouan, spoke much like St. Thérèse of Lisieux.* She, too, had chosen "to sit at the sinners' table," meaning to dwell in hell: that place in us where we have lost contact with the divine Source. "Why have you abandoned me?" cried Christ to the Source of his Being, which he called "my Father and our Father." Yet the Source never abandons us—it is we who lose the sense of its presence, that feeling or per-

---

*[St. Thérèse of Lisieux (1873–1897) was a Roman Catholic nun who was one of three women to be recognized as a Doctor of the Church. She is remembered today for her spiritual memoir, *L'histoire d'une âme* (Story of a Soul). —*Ed.*]

ception of Presence, which Christian theology calls the Holy Spirit: the link and incarnate relation between Son and Father.

What must be renounced is the "sensation" of this Reality, not the Reality itself. Then the Holy Spirit acts in secret, not only unseen by others, but by oneself as well. Sometimes this happens after undergoing those experiences of loneliness, abandonment, and inexpressible consolation, which cannot be imagined by those who have not lived them. "Where are you, my light? Lord, send your spirit!" Staretz Silouan implored constantly.

In a sense, Father Seraphim had also renounced the sensation of the Holy Spirit. Furthermore, he had renounced his own reputation—most of the monks at Mount Athos saw him as a madman, a gyrovague—the worst sort of vagabond monk—who cannot stay in one place nor submit to one set of rules. In his last years he succeeded even in becoming forgotten: today, it is hard to find anyone at Mount Athos who remembers him. Nevertheless, some photos of him still exist, including an extraordinary one, which appeared in a famous Italian album: a luminous face, radiating such simplicity and goodness that his saintliness was striking to any who could see it. Yet when Father Seraphim was approached by any disciple or pilgrim who sought to venerate him, he would drive them away by barking at them ferociously.

This was his way of protecting his space of solitude, dedicated to constant prayer and intercession for all human beings. He passed for a simpleton, a madman, and even for "the shame of the Holy Mountain." He told me that this bad reputation was for him the greatest of victories: "If these men knew the truth of my joy and my suffering before the unbearable paradox of the crucifixion, they would flee Christianity. God has not called me to edify nor to teach the true doctrine. He has asked me to offer him all my breath, all my blood, all my thoughts . . . These men do not need to know how much I love them. What is important is that I really give my life for them."

A certain number of tests had to be passed before anyone (who was not already repulsed or frightened by him) could get close to him. I shall not recount my own tests here, for I have done that elsewhere.[1] But I can sum them up by saying that my own pretensions of spirituality suffered a heavy blow—for Father Seraphim was appalled by anyone who aspired to make a career of spirituality.

"Who are we to judge or instruct others?"

"But in that case, how can I transmit the tradition to another?" I asked.

"There are only two living thirsts who meet, and then walk together toward the Source. Never call anyone 'Father' or 'Master', for there is only one Father and one Master: Reality. And there is no reality but Reality. We pray so as to never forget What Is and Who Is. We invent nothing, we do not seek extraordinary psychic states. This is our only true happiness—it makes no difference whether it is a pleasurable or a painful one. In God there is no more 'I like this' no more 'I don't like that.' There is What Is; that is all. If you are really interested in the whole, it is already here. So why search for it? Is there any place where Reality is not?"

I had heard similar words from sages in India, from Sufis, Lamas, and Roshis of the East. I had also read such things in great texts of Western mysticism. But all my readings, my voyages, and even my clinical death experience in Istanbul, where I felt I discovered that which never dies, only made Father Seraphim chuckle softly or else bark at me.

"Oh yes! Monsieur has read, Monsieur has traveled, yet Monsieur does not know who God is! He has bathed in the Holy Spirit; he has shed tears for the whole world—but only in his dreams! Monsieur has only encountered ideas and idols of God. What does he know of the Reality?"

This is indeed the trap. Whether our language is that of ultimate Reality, *satori, nirvana,* heavenly bliss, or whatever, the problem is that no matter how rich our concepts and our little collection of spiritual experiences, we still have not realized *what is.* We are not real, and our life is worth no more than what our dreams are worth, however beautiful or difficult.

Henceforth, the only question for me became: "How?" How to realize it? What can I do, so that the Christ is no longer an idol for me, a sublime image that illumines me only from the outside?

After many rebuffs, Father Seraphim finally allowed me to accompany him in his wanderings around the holy mountain. But I had to keep my distance, with long stays near Saint Panteleimon or the small monastery of Saint Anne.

"Who am I to teach you? Can't you see that I'm a dog? I bark, I bite and am bitten, like a mad dog that has lost his master and his mind, howling the Holy Name at the moon so as to drown out the noise of his own thoughts . . .

"And you—who are you to pretend to pray? Don't even speak of the prayer of the heart until you have learned to meditate like a mountain." He pointed toward an enormous boulder.

"Ask that stone how it prays. Then come back to me when you know how to pray as hard and as deeply as the Earth and all its stones."

Thus began my initiation into Hesychast meditation and the transmission of the Spirit in which it is to be practiced.

If we must resume the practice in a few steps, we would have to emphasize the importance of the following:

1. Posture. *To meditate is to have a good posture.*
2. Orientation, both external and internal, with a straight spine. *To meditate is to be properly oriented.*
3. Breathing. To go the very end of the exhalation, to allow the inhalation to come of itself. *To meditate is to breathe deeply, and "en pneumati."*
4. Invocation: the Name of Yeshua or a short invocation that calms the mind and gathers our dispersed thoughts. *Meditation is the invocation of the name, which brings peace.*
5. To discover our center. In the Judeo-Christian tradition, this is the heart, the meeting place of the mental (which needs to descend) and the vital (which needs to ascend). A life without a center is a life without meaning. To see and act from the heart. *To meditate is to be centered.*

6. To be unafraid of silence and solitude—not in order to live apart from others, but to join them inwardly by the bond, which unites all that lives and exists (*Logos*) and communicates peace to all (*Hesychia*). *To meditate is to be capable of silence and solitude.*

7. Patience and repetition. These are necessary if we are to become simple and naturally open by the grace of the Holy Spirit, for meditation is a practice that requires strong motivation, great patience, and perseverance. *To meditate is to be patient and to persevere.*

8. The experiences, which accompany meditation, are not to be sought for themselves. Beyond all the psychic effects, which may accompany an assiduous practice (heat, light, tears, surges of joy and pain, and so forth), the spiritual effects are far more important: transfiguration, understanding the meaning of scriptures, Hesychia, peace, a plenitude independent of circumstances, humility, and love of our enemies. This humility and love of our enemies are the realization of the "lineage" in us. In the Spirit that unites Father and Son, we become *alter christus,* another Christ (as St. Gregory said of those he baptized). Thus we become "a further incarnation," inasmuch as our own feelings become those of Christ, and we participate through compassion in the salvation and well-being of all that lives. *Meditation is for the salvation and well-being of all that lives.*

THREE

# THE PRACTICE OF HESYCHAST MEDITATION

## POSTURE

First, I must emphasize the importance of the Staretz, the spiritual father or master. He is a father whose children and disciples are not his, but God's. His role is to transmit the tradition and give his blessing to the practice of those who put their trust in him.

Though nothing is possible without the grace of an authentic transmission, neither is anything possible without the freedom and effort of those who commit themselves to the path of this practice.

Father Seraphim first insisted on proper posture (so as to combat imposture, he might have said). This importance given to a physical position may come as a surprise, especially in the West, where this dimension has often been forgotten. Yet in a religion whose teaching centers around holy incarnation, it is only logical to accord proper importance to the body and its attitudes. The body is not the tomb of the soul, but the temple of the Spirit, the place where the "Word is made flesh."

Hence the first instruction given to one who embarks upon this way is not intellectual, or even spiritual, but physical: "Sit down, and sit like a mountain!" To sit like a mountain means to descend, to acquire gravity, to take root . . . Meditation is not a takeoff, but a landing, a rediscovery of one's ground, and one's roots: to be present with all one's weight, in stillness.

Father Seraphim also instructed me to sit with my pelvis slightly higher than my knees. To facilitate this, he gave me a cushion stuffed with grass, which would also serve as my pillow and my seat for my meals, which I ate in solitude. Its covering was made of the same black cloth as the robes that are worn by Orthodox monks and priests. More or less round, it was thick enough so that I could sit on it cross-legged without pain or fatigue for two or three hours, in a posture that was neither stiff nor casual. Of course this was not the case at first, when the very command to begin my sitting meditation was enough to make me crave to move about restlessly, or even to flee. But we all learn that the body's attitude conditions that of the mind as well. A still and silent body engenders a still and silent heart.

To sit like a mountain is also to alter one's experience of time, for nature's rhythms are very different from our habitual ones.

"Eternity is behind you, and eternity is in front of you," Father Seraphim told me. "If you hold fast to the center, then eternity will be within you. From there, you can take root in the sky, as well as in the Earth. Only one stone is needed to start building a church. Be like that stone, and the Christ will build his Church in you and upon you."

I was greatly helped by the memory of two Romanesque churches I knew in France: Senanque and Le Thoronet. From the outside there is nothing spectacular about them, unlike the later Gothic style. The simple forms of their stones fit harmoniously with the surrounding countryside. But inside—what a magnificent, awe-inspiring space, with its splendid equilibrium and graceful arches, a foundation for the highest silence! These spaces inspired me to seek a "Romanesque" sort of posture. I also thought of certain sculptures of Mary, dating from this period, with her straight spinal column and impeccable sitting posture. On her lap, against her belly and breasts, sits the God-Child, also in an upright meditative posture, with a clear, direct regard, and without the least childish flaccidity. *Sedes sapientiae,* the seat of Wisdom, was the way people described these Virgins. This was what I must try to become: a living mountain, a space-temple, a place where wisdom could sit in repose.

I spent several weeks in this meditation. The most difficult part was to remain hours and days "doing nothing." I was relearning how to be. To simply be, seeking no goal or particular advantage.

To allow Being itself to meditate in me . . . It knows how to do this in stones, not only in gems or in temple stones, but just as much in the small granite outcropping on the flank of the sun-bleached mountain before me.

To meditate like a mountain changes not only the rhythm of our thoughts, but of our judgments. It means to be what we are throughout all weathers, hot or cold, dry or wet, allowing the seasons to pass, and to either erode us or cause us to flower. To see without "judging" is to grant the right to exist to all that moves, grows, crawls, or runs on the mountain. It is to remain solid and unshakable before all the blows, mockeries, or ecstasies of those who pass by.

However, this practice could sometimes lead me into a certain indifference, almost a kind of hardness. It was at these moments that Father Seraphim would begin to assail me with blows. In the beginning I dared not react, but I quickly got the message: I was not made of granite or of marble.

"Meditation should ground you, stabilize you, and root you like mountains. However, your goal is not to become a dead stump but a living human being." Then he took me by the arms and led me into a garden where flowers bloomed among wild herbs.

"Now, you will no longer meditate like a sterile mountain. Learn to meditate like a poppy. But don't forget that you are also the mountain on which the poppy can grow."

## ORIENTATION

To meditate with good posture—that is the first step. Then one must pay attention to one's "orientation." In the Orthodox tradition, one speaks of *philocalia,* or love of beauty. The body, heart, and mind of the meditator must be "oriented toward the beautiful." If this inner and outer direction is lost, then there is disorientation: loss of the orient.

Using the concrete image of the poppy, Father Seraphim wanted me to understand that I must be like a flower or a tree—turning toward the light—the invisible beauty, which surrounds us and is the source of all the other, visible beauties. If the tree does not rise toward the light, it will rot and loose its roots.

"The tree or the flower is your spinal cord. The Tree of Life is planted in the center of the garden. Keep yourself upright. If your roots are deep, it is in order to nourish your ascent toward the light. The light is not only above you, but also before you, and behind you. Stay upright in this space of light like the poppy, which blushes at the sight of the sun."

I mentioned to him that in the Orthodox texts of the *Philokalia,* I had read that a monk should be bent, looking toward his navel, and that this seemed like a painful posture. He looked at me mischievously. "That was for the strong ones of the old days. They were brimming with energy, and they needed to learn a little humility, and be reminded of their limits. They typically held their chests so high, so it was not a bad thing to have them bend a little during meditation. But you are not like them—the state of your spine makes you tend to lean forward, as if you might fall. You need more energy. That is why you must be vigilant about sitting upright in meditation. Keep yourself straight in the light, but without any pride. Besides, if you observe the poppy carefully, it will not only teach you how to have an upright spine, but also how to be supple when the wind blows. Above all, it will teach you great humility."

Indeed, the teaching of the poppy was also in its fleeting impermanence and fragility. One must learn to flower; yet one must also learn to wilt. Now I understood better the words of the prophet: "All flesh is like the grass, and its delicacy is like that of wildflowers. The grass dries up, the flower wilts [ . . . ] the nations are like a drop of water on the edge of a bucket [ ... ] the judges of the earth [ ... ] hardly are they planted, barely have their stems taken root in the earth [ ... ] then they dry up, and the storm carries them away like a wisp of straw" (Isaiah 40:6–24).

If the mountain teaches us a sense of Eternity, the poppy shows us even more about the fragility of time. To meditate is also to know the Eternal in the fleeting moment—a moment that is nevertheless upright, and well oriented. It teaches us that we must flower in the time we are given to flower, to love in the time that is given us to love, unconditionally. The poppy teaches us to accept that we know neither why, for what purpose, nor for whom the poppies flower.

"Love is its own reward," as Saint Bernard said. And "The rose flowers because it flowers, without a why," as Angelus Silesius said.

When I began to "philosophize" a bit about my experiences, Father Seraphim had me follow him down a steep path to the edge of the sea, along a small, dry creek.

"Stop ruminating like a cow over the wisdom of the poppy! Now, let your heart also be a sailor: learn to meditate like the ocean."

## BREATHING

I walked up to the sea. I had acquired good posture, grounding, and orientation. So what was lacking? What could the splashing sound of these waves teach me?

The wind came up, the ebb and flow of the surf became deeper, and this suddenly awakened in me the memory of the ocean. The old monk had not told me to meditate like the sea, but like the ocean. How could he have known of my discovery long ago when I was a child, but forgotten until now? I had spent many hours on the shores of the Atlantic, especially at night, learning to synchronize the rhythm of my own breathing with the rhythm of the great breathing of the waves. I breathe in, I breathe out ... and then, I am breathed in and I am breathed out. I let myself be carried by the breath, carried by the waves ... I was surfing this rhythm of oceanic respiration. Sometimes this practice had brought me into strange trances, on the verge of fainting or dissolving. But this drop of water, which in those days could only "dissolve" in the ocean, was now capable of maintaining its form, its consciousness. Was this because of my new posture and my grounding? No longer was I carried away by the deeper rhythm of my respiration with the sea. The drop of water kept its identity, and yet it knew itself to be one with the ocean. This is how I learned that meditation is a deep breathing that allows the ebb and flow of the breath to be.

I also learned that in spite of all the surface waves, the vast depths of the ocean remain calm. Thoughts come and go, they splash us with foam, but the ground of being remains still. Meditation begins with the wave, which I am, but opens itself to the loss of all sense of a separate ground, taking root in the fathomless depths of the ocean.

Each day this became a little more alive in me, and I recalled the words of a poet who had influenced me as an adolescent:

> *Existence is a sea, constantly full of waves.*
> *Ordinary people see only the waves.*
> *But see how they arise from the depths, beyond number.*
> *The sea is hidden in the waves.*

Today the sea appears to me less "hidden" in the waves. The unity of all things seems more evident, and this unity does not obliterate multiplicity. I have less need to set ground against form, the invisible against the visible. All this constitutes the unique ocean of life.

Is not the ground of my breath the same as *ruakh, pneuma, spiritus*—the great breath of God?

"Whoever listens attentively to their breathing is not far from God," Father Seraphim told me. "Listen to the end of your exhalation, where you can also find the source of your inspiration." Indeed, there were several seconds of the deepest silence, more profound than the ebb and flow of the surface waves—something, which seemed to carry the entire ocean . . .

How could this kind of attention to the breath fail to remind me of Zen and other Buddhist meditation practice? Was it not just this kind of grounding in attention to the breath that brought the Buddha to awakening? I breathe in gently, I breathe out gently, I observe. This is a universal practice—breathing is not just for Buddhists and Christians!

When Jesus told the Samaritan woman to enter into awareness of her breath (*pneuma*), he meant to bring her attention to the very Source of all life, and the place where this meditation is practiced—be it mountain or temple—is not what is important. Father Seraphim placed the highest emphasis on this practice. "It is the essence of Hesychasm. To pray does not mean to think about God. When you are with someone, you breathe with them, you don't think about them. To pray is to breathe deeply and consciously, not to have sublime thoughts about God, but to become one with his *Pneuma* (Holy Spirit), which moves through you.

"Our life hangs only by a breath. It is the thread that links you to the Father, the Source, which brought you into being. Be conscious of this thread, and go where you will."

## INVOCATION

"To be well-seated, upright, and oriented toward the light, to breathe like an ocean . . . yet this is not all there is to Hesychast meditation," Father Seraphim told me. "Now you must also learn to meditate like a bird."

He led me into a small cell near his hermitage, where two doves had made their nest. The cooing of these small creatures was charming at first, but soon became annoying, for they chose precisely those moments when I started to comfortably doze off to begin their tender cooing again.

I asked Father Seraphim about the meaning of this spectacle, and how long it might last. I had no problem meditating with the mountain, the ocean, or the poppy (though some might wonder what all this had to do with Christianity), but to take this languid avian couple as my meditation teachers was more than I could understand!

He explained that in the Old Testament, meditation is indicated by the Hebrew root *haga,* most often rendered as *melete,* or *meletan* in Greek, which becomes *meditari,* or *meditatio* in Latin. In its primitive sense, this root means "to murmur softly," yet it is also used for a variety of animal cries, such as the roaring of the lion (Isaiah 21:4), the chirping of the swallow, and the cooing of the dove (Isaiah 28:14), as well as the growling of the bear.

"On Mount Athos, there are no bears. This is why I have brought you to the dove. But the teaching is the same. You must meditate with your throat, not just as a passage for the breath, but also as an instrument for murmuring the name of God, day and night. When you are happy, you often hum or murmur words or sounds of no significance, barely realizing you are doing it. This murmur causes your whole body to vibrate with a simple and serene joy.

"To meditate is to murmur like the dove, allowing this chant to rise from its source in the heart, just as you have learned to allow the perfume of the flower to arise in you. . . . To meditate is to breathe while chanting. Here is an exercise for you to try, but for now we will not emphasize its meaning: repeat, in a murmuring, humming voice, these words, which are in the heart of all monks on Mount Athos: *Kyrie eleison, Kyrie eleison, Kyrie eleison . . .*"

This proposal did not exactly thrill me. I was already very familiar with these words, translated as "Lord, have mercy," chanted in many masses, marriages, and funerals. Father Seraphim smiled at this. "Yes, that is one of the meanings of this invocation. But there are many others. It also means, 'Lord, send your Spirit!' Or 'May your kindness be with me and with us all . . . May your name be blessed' . . . and so forth. But do not try too much to grasp the meaning of this invocation. It will reveal itself without your seeking it. For now, just be sensitive and attentive to the vibration that it arouses in your body and in your heart. Try to harmonize it peacefully with the rhythm of your breathing. When thoughts disturb you, come gently back to this invocation, breathe more deeply, hold yourself upright, and keep still. Then you will discover the beginning of Hesychia, the peace, which God gives without measure to those who love Him."

After several days, the *Kyrie eleison* became more familiar to me. It accompanied me everywhere, like the buzzing of a bee as it goes about its task of making honey. I did not always move my lips when repeating it. In this case, the vibration became deeper, more inward. Having given up all thinking about its meaning, it sometimes led me into an unknown silence, and I felt like the apostle Thomas when he discovered the resurrected Christ: Kyrie eleison, "my Lord is my God."

The invocation drew me little by little into an intense atmosphere of respect for all that exists, but also of worship for what lies hidden at the root all these existences.

All traditions, seen in the era in which we are living as the end of a cycle of humanity, also agree that in such a time, the best hope for salvation lies in a meditation upon the Name. It is the method best adapted to human beings of the last days of this cycle, the surest way . . .

According to the prophet Joel, "When the sun is turned into darkness, and the moon into blood [ . . . ] whoever calls on the name of Yahweh will be saved."

In Sufi tradition, it is said that a human being who lives in the end times will not be able to accomplish more than a tenth of the law, and this tenth is the invocation of the Name.

In Hindu tradition, the Vishnu-Dharma Attara clearly states: "What one obtains in the first age (of gold) through silent meditation, and in the following ages by sacrifice and devotion, one obtains in the last age (of iron) by celebrating Keshava (Vishnu), and finally, in the Kali-Yuga (the darkest age) by repetition of the Name of Hari, so as to destroy all errors."

Sri Ramakrishna went so far as to say: "The Dharma is the unceasing remembrance of God. It is the law appropriate for this age."

Certain schools of Buddhism also consider the present age as one in which we must repent of our transgressions, cultivate virtue, and pronounce the name of the Buddha Amitabha.

In a world strewn with obstacles and subtle temptations, Buddha advised, "to concentrate upon the recitation of the Name."

We could cite many more similar references. From the Koran, for example: "Remember me, and I will remember you. [ . . . ] The invocation of God is the greatest of all things."

The Desert Fathers of Egypt and Syria had been saying this, as did the Mahabharata long before: "Of all human actions, the highest is invocation (*japa*)."

The Shiva-Samhit adds: "Through repetition of the mantra, one gains beatitude in this world and in the beyond . . . When received from a Master, the mantra must be recited with great care, with neither haste nor languor, with a heart full of confidence and attention, while meditating upon its secret."

In his beautiful book about Mount Athos, Jean Biès notes: "In India, it is said that invoking the Name is preferable even to donning a monk's robes, or joining a religion."

In Semitic traditions, the Name is also Presence and Energy. Hence one must be careful about what one invokes; for just as we become what we love, or become what we think, we also become what we invoke.

In Greek Orthodox monasteries, the invocation is generally Kyrie eleison (in Russian, *Gospodi pomijul* or *pomiloui*). Before introducing me to a higher and more silent practice, closer to the Abba, which for Jesus was the "prayer of the heart," Father Seraphim advised me to dwell for a long time on the Name of Yeshua. It was partly because this name contains the four letters of the sacred tetragrammaton YHWH, the unspeakable Name of Who Is What He Is. It was also because, for him, as for Maximus the Confessor, this Name was "an archetype of synthesis." It is the Name of God and the name of man in one name, the Archetype of encounter between the divine and the human, the infinite and the finite, time and eternity.

"By invoking the name of Yeshua with your breath, you will remember both humanity and divinity. There is no God without humanity, and there is no humanity without God. The name of Yeshua brings you down to earth and raises you up to heaven. In him, nothing is separate, this Name creates balance, it furthers integration, and synthesis in you. It is the instrument that God has given us today for our theosis (divinization).

"You can invoke the Name and simultaneously visualize its Face. This is the function of the icons, which inspire the vision of this face in you. The icon, together with the Name, leads you toward the sovereign Presence, which could 'reign' in your heart. You have learned to meditate like a mountain, like a poppy, like an ocean, like a dove—now you can begin to meditate like a human being: like Abraham."

## CENTERED IN THE HEART

Until now, the teaching of the Staretz had been natural and therapeutic. The monks of ancient times, according to Philo of Alexandria, were also called therapists. Before leading someone toward awakening, their role was to first heal the nature before them, to bring about the best conditions for it to receive grace. For grace is not something apart from nature—on the contrary, it restores and fulfills it.

This was what Father Seraphim was doing with me, teaching me a method of meditation, which some would categorize as a purely natural one. The mountain, the poppy, the ocean, the doves, were all elements of nature, all remind us that we cannot go far until we first recapitulate the three major realms that compose the macrocosm: mineral, vegetable, and animal. Many individuals have lost touch with the cosmos, with stones, animals, and plants. This typically gives rise to all kinds of disease, insecurity, and anxiety. Such an individual is "self-conscious" in the pathological sense of the word, a stranger to the world.

To meditate is first to enter into an awareness and praise of the universe. According to an old Orthodox proverb, "All things knew how to pray before us." Human individuality is the place where the prayer of the world becomes conscious of itself. We are here to name that which other creatures can only stammer. To meditate like Abraham is to enter into a new and higher consciousness called faith. This means holding to the intelligence at the heart of this "Thou" or "Thee," which is symbolized by the familiar second-person form, addressable between all fellow creatures. Such are the experience and the meditation of Abraham: behind the twinkling of the stars, there is something more than stars; a Presence difficult to name, yet which goes by every name.

This is felt in the heart. Something that is more than the universe, yet, which cannot be grasped outside the universe. The difference between Nature and God is the same as that between the blue of the sky, and the blue in the glance of an eye. Beyond all colors, Abraham was in search of this look.

Having learned grounding, rooting, positive orientation toward the light, the peaceful breathing of the oceans, the inner chant, I was thus invited to an awakening of the heart. "Now, suddenly, you are someone." The role of the heart is in effect to personalize all things, including the Absolute, the Source of all that breathes and is. To name it, to call it "My God, My Creator," and to walk in its Presence. For Abraham, to meditate is to maintain contact with this Presence through the most varied appearances.

This form of meditation infiltrates the details of daily life. The episode of the oaks of Mamre shows us Abraham "seated at the entry of the tent, in the heat of the day." From that place, he welcomes three strangers who are later revealed to be messengers of God. "To meditate like Abraham," Father Seraphim told me, "is to practice hospitality. The glass of water you offer to the thirsty does not take you away from silence, it takes you closer to the source of it. To meditate like Abraham, you see, does not just awaken peace and light in you; it also awakens love for all people." And he quoted the famous passage of Genesis, which speaks of Abraham's intercession on behalf of the doomed sinners:

Abraham stood before YHWH, "The One who is and will be." He approached, and said "Will you really destroy the just along with the sinners? Perhaps there are fifty just ones in the city. Are you really going to kill them? Will you not pardon the city for the sake of the fifty just ones within it?" (Genesis 28:23–24)

Little by little, Abraham reduced the number of the just, which would suffice to save Sodom. "May my Lord not be angry with me when I finally say: perhaps only ten just ones might be there?"

This type of meditation frees the heart of all judgment and condemnation, in all times and places. Whatever the horrors that he may have had to witness, he still calls for pardon and benediction.

"To meditate like Abraham takes you even further . . ." this last word was uttered with some difficulty and hesitation by Father Seraphim, as if he had wanted to spare me an experience, which he had undergone, and, which caused a subtle trembling in his memory. But he completed his thought: ". . . it can take you all the way to Sacrifice." Then he quoted the passage from Genesis where Abraham is ready to sacrifice his own son, Isaac. "Everything belongs to God," Father Seraphim continued, murmuring in a low voice. "All is from Him, of Him, and for Him. To meditate like Abraham will lead you to total dispossession of everything you hold dear. Look for what you are most attached to, look for what you are most identified with. For Abraham, it was his only son. If you are capable of this gift, this total self-abandonment, of this infinite confidence in that which transcends all reason and good sense, then all will be returned to you a hundredfold. God will provide."

To meditate like Abraham is to have a heart and a consciousness, which contains nothing other than Him. When he climbed the top of the mountain, Abraham was only thinking of his son. When he came back down, he was only thinking of God.

To pass through the summit of sacrifice is to discover that nothing belongs to "me," for everything belongs to God. This is the death of the ego and the discovery of the Self. To meditate like Abraham is to keep faith in the One who transcends the Universe. It is also to practice hospitality, to intervene for the salvation of all human beings. It is to forget oneself, and to break even the most legitimate attachments, so as to discover oneself, one's kin, and the entire Universe as the dwelling-place of the infinite presence of the One who Is.

In the Zen Buddhist tradition, there is less emphasis on sacrifice, and more on letting go, or detachment. Was it not the supreme detachment that God asked of Abraham? Is not his story also one of letting go, of sacrifice not only of his ego, but even of his "human, all too human" point of view, so as to awaken to another dimension, to awaken to the very heart of Christ within the heart of humanity?

I asked Father Seraphim to speak to me more about Christ in relation to this Awakening of the heart, which is considered the "vital center of the human-divine" in Orthodox tradition. His expression was troubled, as if I had asked an inappropriate question about his secret practice. The greater the revelation one has received, the greater must be the humility, in order to transmit it. Probably he did not feel himself to be humble enough.

Only the Holy Spirit can teach you that [ . . . ] no one knows who is the Son but the Father, and no one knows who is the Father but the Son—and those to whom the Son really wants to reveal it. (Luke 10:22)

"You must become a son in order to pray like the Son, and to meet the One whom he calls his Father and our Father. Only the work of the Holy Spirit can bring you to meet the One on the same terms of intimacy. The Holy Spirit will remind you of all the words of Jesus in such a way that the Gospel comes alive in you, and you will learn to "pray as you should."

But I was not satisfied, and asked him to tell me more. The old man grinned. "Right now, I have an urge to do even worse than bark at you. But you'd only take it as a sign of my saintliness. So I'll tell you again—but more simply.

"To meditate like Jesus is a summation of all the other forms of meditation I've taught you. Jesus is the cosmic human being. I knew how to meditate like the mountain, the poppy, the ocean, the dove, and like Abraham. His heart knew no limits, loving even his enemies and his torturers: "Father, forgive them, for they know not what they do." His hospitality embraced those whom society calls sinners, prostitutes, the sick, the paralyzed, the traitors . . . At night, he retired in secret to pray, and there, like a child, he murmured *abba,* the intimate word for 'father' in his language. It might seem absurd for a man to address the transcendent, infinite, unnamable Absolute, as 'papa.' It's almost ridiculous. Yet it was Jesus's own prayer, and in this simple word, he said it all. Heaven and Earth drew awesomely close. God and man were one. Perhaps one has to actually say 'papa' in the depths of the darkest night in order to understand it. On the other hand, intimate relations between mother or father and their child are not the same thing in our time. They mean nothing compared to what they meant then, so perhaps it's the wrong image for us now . . .

"That's why I prefer to tell you nothing. Better that I offer no image, and wait for the Holy Spirit to fill you with the feelings and the knowledge that were in Christ Jesus, whose abba came not from his lips, but from the depths of his heart. On that day you will begin to understand the Hesychast prayer and meditation."

We must avoid the temptation to compare the value of the prayer of the heart and Zen meditation on the *hara.* What is important is to be centered. As we noted previously, a life without meaning is a life without a center. To act while remaining centered changes everything, both our attitude and our way of being.

In the Hesychast tradition, we are centered in the heart, the place where vitality and thinking are integrated. The heart is the organ of relation, moving from the world of objects to the world of presences. Life is no longer an anonymous energy, but a Presence.

*Whatever your practice or your meditation,*
*ask yourself if this meditation has a heart;*

*then ask yourself if this heart is that of a human being*
*like Abraham; and ask again, if you dare, if this heart*
*is that of a human being in God, or God in a human*
   *being;*
*ask yourself if this heart is that of Christ, or that of the*
   *Love*
*which has just incarnated*
*"for your well-being, and the well-being of all" . . .*

*Part Two*

# THE WAY
## OF COMPASSION

*May all beings be happy, may they be in joy, safety, and health.*

*Everything that is alive, weak or strong, long or short, great, medium, or small, visible or invisible, near or far, born or unborn: may all these beings be happy.*

*May none deceive another, may none despise another, no matter how small.*

*May none wish harm to another, whether through anger, hatred, or ignorance. As a mother risks her life to watch over and protect her only child, may one thus, with a mind without boundaries, cherish all that lives.*

*Love every being with kindness.*

*Love the world in its entirety, above, below, and all around, without limits, with infinite kindness and goodwill. Standing or walking, seated or reclining, whenever one is conscious, it is good and beautiful to cultivate this wish, this vow.*

*This is called the supreme way of life.*

THE METTA SUTTA

In any path of compassion, one never meditates for oneself, for that would limit the benefits of the meditation. One meditates for the welfare of all. The most useful effect is to calm our own mind. If we are truly at peace, then this world has at least one place of peace, and it is communicated to all living beings, and to society in general.

Before presuming to "do good" for others—and we shall see the extent of the ambiguity of this expression—we must be clear about the spirit in which we are acting. The teaching of all great wisdom-traditions urges us to pay attention to our own state of mind and vigilance. Our intentions and our vows can be the best in the world, yet they will not suffice if our mind is not clear and peaceful. The right instrument used in the wrong spirit gives wrong results.

It is important never to separate love and knowledge, compassion and wisdom. A wisdom without compassion is closed upon itself and does not bear fruit. A compassion without wisdom is a madness and a cause of suffering.

# FOUR

# WHAT IS A BODHISATTVA?

*Bodhi,* in Sanskrit, means "awakened intelligence." The Buddha is thus "the awakened intelligence," "awakening," or the state of awakening. The word *sattva* means "being" or "essence." A bodhisattva is thus an "awakened being," a being on the path of awakening, or a being whose state of mind is awakened. Other interpretations are also possible.

In Buddhist tradition, the bodhisattva is one who is totally engaged in the path of awakening and transformation. Such a being wants to clearly see what is; reality as it is. They want this not only for themselves but also for the well-being of all. As long as all beings are not awakened, a bodhisattva cannot be fully awakened, for they are never awakened alone.

But this definition needs some refinement and precision. *A bodhisattva is a being who is undaunted by the multitude of beings who are not free, undaunted by the time, which seems to be needed for all to be free, and would sacrifice their own head and all their limbs in order for this great awakening to happen.* Bodhisattvas are generally considered as beings who, through their asceticism and transformation, have arrived at a state of awakening, but have renounced to enter into the completion of this awakening as long as there is a single being who suffers.

The Christian tradition maintains that one is never saved alone. It is as if someone refused to experience paradise, or to see God, as long as there is one being who does not participate in this vision. "May I be anathema to my brothers," said St. Paul. As long as a single being does not know the uncreated Creator and Love, the foundation of being and life, then perhaps we could say that one renounces, not the knowledge itself, but the savoring of this knowledge in its fullness.

Here, we are speaking of a state of consciousness, which is not of the small "me," but a cosmic state of consciousness, open to all beings. My own body is the body of the universe, and as long as a single being suffers in this universe, I cannot know the fullness—in Christian terms, the beatitude.

Thus I have taken the path of the bodhisattva.

# FIVE

# THE DHAMMAPADA AND THE GOSPELS

How can we fail to see the affinity between the words of Siddhartha Gautama, the Buddha, and those of Yeshua of Nazareth, the Christ? It is neither our intention to mix the Dhammapada with the Gospels, nor to oppose them to each other. We take the middle path, avoiding both syncretism and sectarianism.

As regards Buddhist tradition, I will content myself with transmitting what I received from the Dalai Lama when I met him in the United States, and with what I received in France from his disciple, Kalu Rinpoche, as well as the latter's disciple, Lama Denys Teundroup.

Regarding Christian tradition, I shall echo what I received from part of the Orthodox tradition, especially that of Mount Athos—an unbroken lineage, which goes back to the Desert Fathers, the Church Fathers, and the apostles—as well as my experience with the Roman Catholic tradition, as taught by Dominicans.

Whether we are Buddhist, Christian, or atheist, we are all in search of truth, on the road to awakening. This awakening is not the special province of Buddhists, any more than love is the special province of Christians. Reality is not a possession of anyone. We enter into spirituality from the place where we find ourselves. What is important is to take a step still further, to advance, to become better.

"Is such-and-such a practice better than the other one? What is the right practice for me to follow?" I asked the Dalai Lama.

"Anything that makes you better is right for you," he answered.

What simplicity and good sense! The best religion or practice is the one that makes us better.

It is not my aim in writing this book to suggest that Buddhists are better than Christians, or vice versa. All of us, even atheists, are at heart on a way of trying to become better, and make the world a better place to live in—to act in such a way that life becomes "possible."

If the words of the Buddha resonate with the words of Christ, it is because there is no reality but Reality. The truth for a Buddhist should be the truth for a Christian, and untruth for a Christian should be untruth for a Buddhist. Otherwise, what sort of truth are we talking about? There are different ways of incarnating it, different ways of incarnating life, consciousness, and Love, but there is only one Reality.

We are all on a path toward this Reality, but we may have more affinity with some practice that is more rigorous than another, more devotional. But we must never forget that what is best for us is not necessarily best for another. It is not our place to judge whether others should engage in the same practice we do. But together, we can work toward our transformation and that of the world.

# SIX

# THE VOW OF COMPASSION

What is the vow of a person who is animated by compassion? Is it wise to devote ones life to the welfare of all beings? Is it even rational to make such a vow? Is it not a dream, or even a form of megalomania, to make such a vow? What are the motivations and justifications of this vow, both personal and impersonal?

We might concern ourselves with the welfare of others because we discover that our own welfare is thereby increased. This is not necessarily a bad thing. To open to others is a way of opening our heart, as well as our intelligence. It is perhaps the best means of "going beyond ego." On the path of the bodhisattva there is a very personal motivation: our own liberation. To become free and happy through loving.

There are other, more impersonal justifications. Through the practice of compassion, unconditional love is possible because we have within us this capacity to give because our true nature is Love and Light. In the language of Christianity we say that we have the spirit of Christ, his Breath (Pneuma, the Holy Spirit), his energy. And it is from this Reality "more truly us than we ourselves," that we can work for the welfare of all living beings.

Yet to wish for the welfare of all beings from the ego-space of "I want!" is to risk a narrow limitation, which can well be catastrophic for others. To wish happiness for others according to our own ideas of happiness is to invite difficulties. The quality of being and loving, known as compassion, is never centered on this "me." It is not "me" who loves, because it is precisely this "me" that is incapable of love. With all the lacks and disappointments it has accumulated over a lifetime, this "me" seeks only to perpetuate itself. It constantly demands to be loved, and it never gets enough. Only the Self is capable of true giving and unconditional love.

We must awaken to a quality of being, consciousness, and love, which is our essential nature, to allow it to first manifest within us, and then to allow this capacity of giving and this quality of awakening to grow, so that all our actions are permeated with it.

# SEVEN

# THE PRACTICE OF COMPASSION

It is all too easy to make a vow to be full of goodwill: "Peace on Earth, goodwill toward men . . ." But how does this manifest concretely, in the details of everyday life? What is the practice of a being who has chosen compassion as the rule of life?

Such a practice consists of developing the six perfections in ourselves:

- Giving
- Discipline, mastery of both mind and actions (positive and negative), observation of our own behavior
- Patience
- Energy
- Meditation practice
- Wisdom

To meditate is to set aside a certain time, which presupposes discipline, patience, and much energy. Meditation can lead us to wisdom, to intelligent love and intelligent compassion, which are not harmful. We must repeat: the practice of compassion from a mind, which is unclear and not at peace, can only be harmful. To wish for the welfare of others with a troubled mind does more harm than good. This is why it is important to develop the six perfections in ourselves.

We can bring this practice into resonance with those, which are given in Christian tradition, called *nepsis* in ancient times, which means "vigilant attention." It is also love with clarity. The practice of vigilance requires that our mind be supple, fluid, without fixations. It requires dwelling in openness. If we experience difficulties in our relationships it is because we have certain ideas about others. We fix the personality of the other in their problematic emotions and reactions; and we identify ourselves with a more positive emotion, sensitivity, affection, and intellect.

What Buddhist tradition calls the ultimate *bodhicitta* is the introduction into our lives of moments when we let go of all these fixations, allowing the flow of consciousness and compassion to fill us, instead of fixing things in one form or another.

Certain more advanced practices may appear bizarre to those who are not familiar with them. These include exchanging one's "me" for that of another, inviting into oneself all the negativity and pain of another individual, of a collectivity, or even of the entire universe, so as to transform it. This practice must not be misunderstood as some sort of transcendental masochism where we "experience" the misery of others. That would serve nothing but to increase our own unhappiness. Instead, it is a "breathing in" of another's pain, but with a special state of mind, which is capable of transforming it.

In the *tonglen* practice of Tibetan Buddhism, one breathes in these negativities without opposing them in any way, thereby freeing one of all fear and aversion. And one breathes out total positivity and well-being, giving the best of oneself, the awakening and compassion, which is not "me," but the Living One within me.

This is an alchemical work. One can only help things toward a higher evolution by accepting them, by first taking them into oneself—not to keep them, but to transmute them. This of course requires the presence of this fire of transmutation within us. We welcome even the worst filth, so that it may be transmuted by the fire, which also makes use of our own rotten wood, transforming it into living flames.

The Christian tradition is a way of the "Servant" (see Isaiah): one who takes upon herself the pain, the delusion, the evils, and sins of the world so as to transform them. As with tonglen, there is no trace of any morbidity or masochism here. On the contrary, if we are able to make such a practice our own, it can become the wellspring of our own profound happiness, and that of others as well. But it presupposes that we are able to free ourselves of fear of death, sufferings, and of evils—and that we are able to transform these negativities within ourselves.

It is useful to recall these words of the Buddha, which are the foundation of these later practices of compassion:

Do not believe anything merely because you are told it is so, because others believe it, because it comes from Tradition, or because you have imagined it. Do not believe what your teacher tells you merely out of respect. Believe, take for your doctrine, and hold true to that, which, after serious investigation, seems to you to further the welfare of all beings.

The Buddha emphasizes the importance of direct experience, and the discipline of verifying things for oneself. Things can only fructify or become truly useful to us insofar as we make them our own.

This is also Jesus's meaning, when he says "Come, and see!" In other words, experience it, and find out for yourself! This leads us into a practice, which is not based on belief (there is nothing to believe), but on experience and verification. We must exercise both intelligent observation of everything and concrete verification of that which helps us advance—or not advance.

The Buddha's ultimate criterion of "furthering the welfare of all beings" is a criterion of discrimination. If something furthers only my own welfare, it is not yet truly useful. What I do, what I learn, what I teach—does it further the welfare of all beings? Does it bring a little more peace, happiness, truth, and lucidity to humanity? Or does it add to the confusion, disturbance, and unhappiness that is already there?

Hence the first rule is to experience, verify, and discriminate.

"It is just and good if it furthers the welfare of all beings." This essential teaching of the Buddha cannot arise from an egocentric attitude, but from one, which might be called "allocentric": something is only useful inasmuch as it furthers the welfare of others and the welfare of the universe.

"I only teach two things: the reality of suffering, and the way beyond it," also said the Buddha. We must admit that we are not completely happy. We cannot escape the fact of pain in life, and unhappiness in the world. We must face this truth of suffering, otherwise we remain fixed by it and will never go beyond it. But to merely accept this suffering with no possibility of transforming it changes nothing. On the other hand, to see the possibility of attaining happiness without fully accepting suffering leads only to illusion.

In the Christian tradition, St. Augustine points out that "a thing is necessary insofar as it contributes to freeing us from unhappiness and leading us to ultimate peace." Any activity that does not further our own and all others' salvation is dispensable, unnecessary. The Greek word *soteria,* which has become translated as "salvation," actually means "health"—health of being in the largest sense—liberation of being. For St. Augustine, it is well to ask oneself, before acting, whether it is useful to perform this action. Does it help me to grow, to evolve? Is it useful for others? (These are two fundamental criteria.) If the answer is negative, then it is not useful. I am wasting time, distancing myself from the Real. This distancing, or exile, is suffering and illusion.

"When you are shot in the arm by an arrow, do you demand to know who shot it, and what kind of wood his bow is made of? Or do you take care of the wound?" This was the Buddha's response to the question of the origin of evil and suffering. We are not in this life in order to answer the question of the origin of pain, suffering, and existence, but to see that we are in pain, and find out how to overcome this pain in ourselves and in the world.

Whether or not metaphysics can establish the eternity of the world, there is still birth, old age, misery, mourning, and despair in human life, and what I need to be concerned about is their overcoming in this life. To speculate about the eternity of the world and its origin is not wrong in itself. But first I must ask how to go beyond the suffering in which I find myself. This is my primary task. I have neither the energy nor the time to spare for vain and insoluble metaphysical questions. The best use for my energy and time is for the salvation and well-being of all that lives.

# EIGHT

# IMPURITIES OF THE MIND

W e are what we think, and what we are depends on our state of mind and consciousness. Our thoughts make the world in which we live. Those who speak and act with an unhealthy mind are followed by suffering like the cart that follows the ox who pulls it," says the Dhammapada. On the way of compassion, our attitude is of extreme importance, for the world we live in depends on how we conceive and interpret it. To change the world, we must change our state of mind.

This brings us to the heart of the Gospel and *metanoia*. In Greek, this literally means going beyond the *nous*. It is a change of consciousness so radical that it is called "conversion." In other words: change your thinking, your interpretation of the world, change the way you see! To change the way you see is to change the world.

In daily life, things are what they are. It is the way we see them that makes us happy or unhappy. Likewise, people are what they are, and the way we see them can cause suffering, or on the contrary, can trigger a change for the better, a transformation.

To walk the path of love and compassion is to convert our mind, to transform our seeing, to enter into a process of *metanoia*. Our thought influences the world in which we live—not only our subjective world, but also objective structures as well. Our thought is incarnated in our gestures and actions. If it is not purified and cleaned, our actions cannot be pure, or just.

These moments of meditation and self-observation are not just for ourselves, but for the welfare of all. A sick mind will only add to the misery of the world. Before we can love, we must find a way not to do harm by our thoughts, our state of mind. Respect for others, in this will to do no harm, is surely the first act of love that we can offer them. *Ahimsa,* or nonviolence, can also be translated as harmlessness.

To do no harm is to transform the world, beginning with ourselves, with those thoughts, emotions, and feelings over which we have a certain power. Otherwise, we live in a world of projections, desires, and aversions, which take us over, and thus create more suffering.

As the Buddha said:

O my friends, a garment that is stained and filthy remains filthy, no matter what color it is dyed—blue, yellow, red, or orange. Why? Because the cloth itself is dirty. Likewise, when the mind is impure you can expect bad consequences.

O my friends, when a cloth is clean and pure, then no matter what color it is dyed—blue, yellow, red, or orange—it will remain pure in color. Why? Because the cloth is clean. Likewise, my friends, when the mind is pure, you can expect good consequences.

What are these impurities of the mind?

Greed and craving are impurities of the mind. Malice, anger, ill will, hypocrisy, insult, jealousy, treachery, dishonesty, stubbornness, impetuosity, presumption, arrogance, complacency, and heedlessness are impurities of the mind.

These are our attitudes, and this list reminds us that our mind is not as clear as we might think. If we wish to rediscover our true nature, we must work to become more simple, so as to attenuate and clear away these impurities. They are not who we are. The true *ascesis,* or work of purification, does not consist in trying to change who we are, but to become who we really are. We must let go of all that is not who we are, all those memories that have attached themselves to us, all those experiences that make us react in habitual ways.

This is a path where nothing is to be invented but rediscovered: our true nature. We free our essence from the mass of memories that impedes and obscures it. As long as we cannot see things as they are, we cannot love them as they are. When we claim to love someone, what is it we really love? Typically, it is a projection, an image, a representation that fits with our limited concepts and memories of the past. We make loved ones fit our mold, our limited categories. But we do not love them as they are.

The quality of our love and compassion depends on the quality of our mind and attitude. Wisdom and compassion cannot be separated. In Christian tradition, this is called purifying the heart. If our heart is not pure, our love is not true. This work of purifying the heart was practiced by ancient monks; and the Buddha's list of impurities is the same as that of Evagrius of Pontus, of Johannes Cassianus, and all the Desert Fathers. We must undergo a purification of the heart if our compassion is to be true.

**Question: Is desire an impurity? Is it bad?**
First, we must distinguish the different experiences, corresponding to two different meanings covered by the word "desire." Egocentric desire is for oneself. This is very different from the desire for the welfare of all beings, which is the foundation of the bodhisattva vow!

The noblest desire is surely the desire for the Other as Other. This desire seeks no satisfaction, and is not for oneself. However, there is another type of desire for the other, which consists of demands and needs. Few people have access to the noble desire. In general, what we call "desire" refers to a need or a demand, and this is the sense in which many Buddhist translations use the word. It is not the desire for the happiness of all beings, nor the desire for the Other as Other. The latter is an intimate desire, which sometimes inhabits us, but rarely—precisely because we have so many needs and demands to satisfy, and these desires demand a response.

It is important to enter into those moments of emptiness where we do not think, or where we are not identified with what we think, where we have no opinion of the other. What prevents fluidity in relations with others are the thoughts we have about them. In order to practice compassion, it is essential not to enclose others in our thoughts, at least during certain moments. In this emptiness and availability others can be who they are.

If we have a mind that has not been purified, we can only live in suffering and create suffering. If we speak and act with a whole, clear, sane mind, we can know happiness in itself, and this will be communicated to others. But this does not refer to any sort of happiness! It is not those little happinesses that are dependent on security from response to our needs or demands. Perhaps true happiness is the response to this most intimate and mysterious desire, which causes us to wish for the well-being, the realization, and the freedom of all beings. "May all beings be happy . . ." This Buddhist expression resonates with the Christian prayer: "May all beings be saved. May all know Thee, the Ultimate Reality."

The Christ taught, as did the Buddha: "Before entering into the way of compassion, change your attitude, observe your own mind with vigilance. The quality of what you will be able to do and give to others will depend on this. If not, everything will be more or less poisoned, and poison will be added to poison."

Jesus said: "Judge not, lest you be judged. For you shall be judged by the judgment with which you judge." What does this mean? It means that we enclose the world inside our judgments and our ways of seeing, and it is this that judges us, revealing what we are. Our reactions and judgments are like mirrors in which we can only see ourselves. The other can only be seen by going beyond the mirror.

"A day lived in wisdom and meditation is worth more than ten years lived in ignorance and complacency; a day lived in wisdom and meditation is worth more than a century lived in luxury and vice; a day lived in wisdom and meditation is the best way of furthering the welfare of all living beings." This Buddhist teaching means that the peace of mind, the transparency of our projections, the simplification of our being and attitude, which result from such a day, are not only better for our own soul than ten years lived in ignorance or a century lived in vice—it is also the best thing one can do for the world. In such a day are grown the seeds of peace for all humanity.

In Buddhist tradition, it is also said that one true meditation can erase a lifetime of bad karma. Bad karma is simply the consequences of negative actions accumulated in this life or other lives. It is a weight of memory, which encumbers even our genetic code, and is not necessarily from an individual past life, but from the collective memory of the human race.

Through one simple meditation, one authentic silence, we can lighten this burden of memories and bring liberation and renewal to both our own past and that of humanity. A moment of true meditation can take us out of this chain of causes and effects, out of the time of past/future. Meditation can recenter us around the axis, which is beyond time, and greater than it. The Buddha was emphatic about this point: "Do not be concerned about your past and future lives. Take care of your life in the present moment. Do not be concerned about your past or your future: be concerned about your eternity." Why do we worry so much about our future, and so little about our eternity? As Jesus said, "Neither turn back, nor worry about tomorrow."

Freedom, or awakening, is what brings the story of ourselves, the world, and the universe to turn again around the vertical axis of essential Life. Of course these very terms are still too spatiotemporal. This world freedom is found neither above nor below, but it is an opening of the world of causality, liberating it from the chain of causes and effects, into the world of the unborn, the uncreated. Now we can understand why the Desert Fathers said: "A saint is like a splinter in the flesh of history." The saint is like a wound of light, which prevents the world from closing upon its darkness, which reduces our being to something that is simply going to die. If the world were limited to itself, then there would be nothing but birth, death, and decay. The universe itself is no more than birth, death, and decay, though on a vaster scale—but even if it has five billion years left, it is still just as finite. It still has a beginning and an end.

The role of meditation and of metanoia is to create an opening to the deathless, the uncreated, the eternal within this world of mortality and decay. This may well seem unimaginable, but it is not a matter of trying to imagine it but of opening ourselves to it. Meditation is the means that can allow this Reality to be experienced.

The Buddha said, "Truly, hatred never ceases through hatred, but through love. This is an eternal law." And the Christ: "Love your enemies, and bless them instead of cursing them." This is not a belief to be accepted, but an observation to be verified. Hatred engenders only hatred. On the other hand, love, together with patience, can transform this hatred. The Desert Fathers said: "Conquer anger (be stronger than anger) through love, conquer evil with good, conquer greed with generosity, conquer the liar with the truth." And St. Paul: "Speak the truth, do not be carried away by anger, give the little you possess to one who begs." To this, we might also add the words of Jesus: "If someone asks you to go a mile, go two. If someone tries to take away your tunic, give him your cloak as well." When we are free, neither bound nor rigid, we allow the flow of life and love to run through us. Then the very essence of being is manifest, the essence of the generosity within us. This is an experience well worth living.

"Do not concern yourself with the actions, the faults, or the shortcomings of others. Instead, be conscious of your own actions, your own faults, and your own shortcomings."

"Why do you look at the splinter in the eye of your brother? Can you not see the log in your own eye?"

Whether we read the Dhammapada or the Gospels, we find that there is a Reality to be lived that goes well beyond the limits of common sense.

We poison our own life and worldview when we habitually focus on what is wrong with others. This wrongness then fills us and makes the world and ourselves uglier. Again, it is the image of the mirror, which reflects only the one who stares into it. We become what we see, and we become what we love. Of this, there is no doubt and hence the importance of vigilance toward the orientation of our internal mirror. This is the beginning of practice.

"He insulted me, he struck me, he robbed me, he humiliated me . . ." Those who entertain such thoughts live in resentment and pain. Those who do not entertain such thoughts live in peace. The key word here is *entertain*. If we have been struck, insulted, or humiliated, then this is a fact, beyond our power to change. What is within our power to change is whether or not we entertain thoughts such as: "he struck me, he insulted me, he humiliated me."

We cannot avoid certain painful experiences and events of our existence. Pain is a part of existence. What is important is not to entertain and harbor pain. If we cease to entertain the thoughts and resentments triggered by painful experiences, this pain can fade away.

This can be related to another passage from the Gospels: "Let not your right hand know what your left hand does." This applies both to the pain that happens to us and to the good that we may do. To live our experience without the burden of ego means that there is no "me," which holds on to suffering, thereby adding unnecessary pain. Before performing a good act, the primordial question is: How can this be done so as not to add more suffering and more harm? The source of the harm—that which creates unnecessary suffering—is the "me." It is rooted in thought, which elaborates upon the event itself.

There is a proverb of elegant simplicity in Latin: *Est est, non est non est.* Translated into English: "What is, is; what is not, is not." An implication of this is: "Let your yes be yes, let your no be no." Similar words are attributed to the Christ. Six centuries before him, the Buddha used the same terms to define *nirvana:* "To see things as they are; that is, that is; that is not, that is not."

The way of compassion is that of a man or woman who is serious about the quest for freedom from suffering, and a happiness not only for oneself, but also for others. It is a way for those who seek to free themselves of egoistic habits, which consist of seeing everything in relation to oneself, a "self" that can never be satisfied and always wants and demands more.

# NINE

# THE FIVE MOTIVATIONS

## THE "DESIRE FOR THE GOD-REALMS"

When we first become interested in a spiritual path, we want to be free of uneasiness and suffering. Something feels wrong, and we don't know what its real cause is. After being disappointed by other forms of seeking, we try a more spiritual way, which will perhaps really free us from suffering. Perhaps we will suffer less if we concern ourselves more with others and less with ourselves. Perhaps we have taken a wrong turn in focusing only on ourselves, which leaves us dissatisfied. We begin to sense that happiness does not depend only upon our small selves, that it is part of a consciousness that is infinitely more vast. But in this motivation, we are not yet free of an egocentric attitude: we lack happiness and peace of mind. Therefore, we seek to fill this lack.

In Tibetan Buddhism, this first motivation is "desire for the god-realms," a nostalgia for a lost paradise. This nostalgia is not unrelated to the memory of the undifferentiated bliss of the maternal womb. This feeling of lack functions as a need. We long for this paradise, symbolized by the realm of the peaceful deities in the Tibetan tradition, a place without worry and problems. This motivation is legitimate. But it is only a first step.

## THE DESIRE FOR AWAKENING

Subsequently, our motivation may become deeper, more refined. Beyond the desire for a happiness, which is not present, beyond the desire for nonsuffering, for peace, for the personal happiness of a "me," which by now may have attained certain insights, there is revealed in us a desire for evolution, for awakening. At this point we become aware of something in us, which will lead us to a greater happiness than we had imagined. As soon as we enlarge the tent of our abode, the ego becomes more porous, more open.

This experience also has a physical aspect. For example, when you have back pain, and someone places their hands on your back, saying, "give me your suffering, go beyond the limits of your body," you may feel your pain diminish immediately, as if freed from imprisonment in the limits of your body. This is something worth recalling when one accompanies a person who is sick or dying. In offering them, through our presence and contact, an opening of their ego and their body-identification, we allow something in them to loosen, to open to well-being and relief.

To be grounded in an attitude of compassion is to be capable of receiving and welcoming the suffering, which the other is giving us. This does not mean that we suffer for them, but that we offer them the possibility of going beyond the separate self in which suffering is harbored.

## "DISINTERESTED" DESIRE

The third motivation is the same as the desire for awakening, but without any concern for personal perfection. For the desire to be free of ego is still a desire of the ego. The separate self wants to be a better separate self! This sometimes reaches caricatural proportions in those who consider themselves as spiritually advanced: "I no longer have an ego!" This is what is meant by "spiritual materialism" or "subtle inflation." The separate self takes itself for the Self, like a flea that imagines itself to be an elephant.

With the third motivation, one has let go even of the desire to be without ego, to feel happy, or to experience awakening. Though it is right and proper to begin the path with such desires, the more one advances, the more one notices that the very fact of wanting to be happy is an obstacle to true happiness, and that wanting to experience awakening can be the very thing that is preventing our awakening.

It is in the very heart of the desire for happiness and freedom from suffering that we discover that the desire for the ultimate happiness of awakening is still self-centered, and that our idea of what happiness and awakening are, can be the obstacle that prevents us from tasting them here and now. The bodhisattva is always grounded in this inner truth, yet without any concern for his or her own awakening, realization, or perfection. The goal is still awakening, but stripped of all personal advantage. It is an awakening, which makes itself available for others. Is it possible to seek awakening without desiring any personal benefit from it? It is rare for us to live in such spontaneous detachment, and our motivation is always mixed in the beginning.

## GRATUITY

A moment arrives when we experience true, spontaneous pleasure in doing things for others, with no thought for oneself. In this desire there is something, which does not seek fulfillment for itself, or even for happiness. This is the desire for the other in their pure otherness. Here, we touch the very essence of a desire, which is profoundly human and almost divine. This goes beyond the limits of the ordinary "self." In our habitual mode of doing things, we are kind to others because we want them to be kind to us, a kind of quid pro quo. But as soon as we begin to operate outside this mode, there is a mutation of the mind, a spiritual transformation of the heart, which enables us to act gratuitously to help others with no concern for ourselves.

The goal is to awaken this motivation within us, to enter little by little into this vow. When we help someone we can rarely resist a kind of self-satisfaction ("I did something good!"), which can be extremely subtle. The bodhisattva changes all this, saying, in effect: "I did it gratuitously, for no reason, out of pure love for a being, allowing Life to inhabit me." Here is where we encounter the quality of gratuity, which is of a higher order. When confronted with a difficult or disagreeable act, to remember that we are doing it freely, expecting nothing, calls forth a quality of energy in us, which is not that of the ego, or of what we call our "self."

In Buddhist tradition, one does good so as to have good karma. Negative actions result in negative consequences, and doing harm to others results in doing harm to oneself. "As you sow, so shall you reap," as the New Testament says. The harm, evil, and unhappiness that we sow will return to us someday, even if the immediate consequences are those of success. This can be verified by examining our lives: unjust acts come back to us, though it may be years later, and the pain of these consequences will increase until we accept transformation.

This is still the first motivation. The positive or negative energy of our actions is not lost, but returns to us. Kind, patient, and generous actions build a good karma, so as to prepare a rebirth in a better world, or perhaps to leave space-time and worlds of cause and effect entirely, so as to return to the beatitude of *nirvana,* the state of pure, clear light. But all these motivations are still self-interested, however subtle. Nevertheless, they cannot be denied, for they are grounded in the logic of the laws of cause and effect.

## SHARING

There is still another category of self-interested motivation: "If all living beings could know the fruits of the ultimate reward of generosity as I know them, they would never cease giving to others and sharing everything with them, even their last morsel of food." The Buddha uses the example of food, but one could just as well speak of any possessions. When I do not share what I have, I cannot even taste the essence of having it. I may be happy alone, but not as much. My happiness is increased by sharing it with another. I may be able to exult alone in the beauty of a landscape; I may be able to live without others, but perhaps not as well . . .

It is possible to work out one's liberation alone, but it will be less intense than one that is shared with others. The Buddha himself noted that this openness to others is one of the conditions of our happiness and our development in this life and in others to come. He does not appeal directly to the inner quality of gratuity, but he does list a certain number of considerations, which express how much helping others is the same as helping oneself. To love your neighbor as yourself is to treat them as not other than yourself. It is as if we were organs of a single body, where helping one part helps all parts. This vision is not egocentric, not enclosed in a separate self.

# TEN

# THE FOUR CONSIDERATIONS TAUGHT BY THE BUDDHA

## THE SAME FAMILY

This first consideration is perhaps the strangest to the Western mind: this person whom I have a tendency to dislike and perhaps even hate, could well have been my mother in a previous life. In fact, it is difficult to find any being who has not been my mother, father, son, daughter, brother, or sister in some previous life! Here, we are in a social context where high values are placed on family ties, which are a symbol of preciousness.

When the Buddha uses the example of a mother's love and care for her child as a symbol of the bodhisattva nature it is because maternal love is the best example of gratuity, or unconditional love. A mother wants her child to be well, and she wants this in a totally natural and spontaneous way. Of course we can find plenty of examples of selfish mothers who see their children as objects for their own fulfillment. Sometimes this motivates the very desire to have children in the first place, and parents often want their children to give them a love, which they did not receive from their own parents, creating a vicious chain . . .

When Buddhist teachings use the symbol of a mother or father, they mean a truly good mother or father. Such an image may be problematic, or even painful, for those who have not experienced such parental love. We must bear in mind that when the Buddha says, "Be kind to this person, because he or she may have been your mother," it means to do no harm to someone who fundamentally wants only the greatest good for you, regardless of appearances.

**Question: If we know that an action we do for others is also advantageous for us, does not this diminish the good we do for them?** We must accept both truths: that it is good for us and good for them. Why set these truths up against each other? Are we not moving toward a reality where self and other are no longer separate? We must allow ourselves to experience this reality step-by- step.

There is a moment when the wall between self and other dissolves. That is when the question itself is seen to be illusory. How can there be a problem when the same life animates both bodies? To truly do good for another is always to do good for oneself—and vice versa. This is when we experience the self as linked to the entire universe.

We are linked, and interlinked. Even contemporary physics speaks of the interconnection of all things. To truly do good to one part of the universe is to do good to all of it. To nourish a tree is to nourish my vegetal nature. We are not separate beings. To destroy the environment is to destroy ourselves and our world. To injure a blade of grass can disturb a star. This is no longer just poetry; it is now physics as well.

The Buddha's argument is a bit different from this. He appeals to sensitivity, to personal familial feelings, never imagining a type of mother who harms her children. When he urges his disciples to see each being they encounter as their mother, he is teaching that all beings are of one cosmic family.

Compassion is intimately related to the feelings of a mother or a father. Nevertheless, we can arrive at the same conclusion (i.e., that we are all of one great family) without having to imagine that someone as our mother, son, and so forth, or to resort to doctrines of reincarnation. I remember hearing a man say once that he had "discovered" that his wife had been his sister in a previous life. Instead of pleasing him, this upset him to the point that he wanted to divorce her: "I must choose someone who is truly my wife!"

Teachings of reincarnation may solve some things, but they can also complicate them. The essence of the Buddha's teaching is not about reincarnation, but about our interrelatedness and our unity. He wanted to convey this by awakening feelings of kinship toward strangers in us. Family feelings toward others normally (barring pathological cases) indicate an attitude of being unable to wish them harm.

## A COMMUNITY OF DESTINY

The second consideration, which the Buddha taught as an aid in pursuing the way of compassion, is that of sharing the same destiny. What I experience, others may also experience. What others endure and suffer may be felt by me, because I am subject to the same human frailties, and I have endured the same pain, violence, death, and absurdity as have they. I can understand them, because we share the same destiny.

Nothing human is strange to us. The depth of our compassion is proportional to the depth of our living. It is my belief that those who have true self-knowledge do not judge others, because they have seen the sources of crime and dishonesty in themselves. When another commits a crime or lies, they do not condemn them, for they see this as a potential fault, which is part of being human, and sometimes gets the upper hand.

"Who has not suffered, cannot understand." There is a grain of truth in this proverb. One must have experienced hunger in order to really know what it is, one must have experienced being locked up to know the pain a prisoner feels, one must have seen the potential madness in oneself in order to know the suffering of the insane. Like knows like.

The best therapists are those who have known illness and then recovered their health. But it is not the fact that they have suffered that changes things. If someone tells you they are in pain, and you answer, "So am I," it does not help them. We do not help a floundering swimmer to reach the shore by drowning with them! What is necessary is to meet another where they are, and to welcome their suffering, so as to be more capable of offering them some of the healing power that has helped us. Thus we offer them, not our suffering, but some of the power, which has enabled us to swim to the other shore, to suffer less than they, and to know more peace in the very heart of absurdity.

"Consider others as like yourself. Do no harm." This teaching from the Dhammapada is also that of the Gospels.

## IMPERMANENCE

The third consideration, which, according to the Buddha, can make us more compassionate, is the perception of the fundamental impermanence of our existence. We are fragile beings, passing through a world that is itself impermanent. Why make such a fuss over that which will not endure? My bank account will not weep at my funeral. As we become less and less rigid in our attachments, we become free, capable of giving and receiving.

This experience of impermanence, which we all share, can awaken a certain sense of humor in us, giving us a perspective of distance from all that happens. We can not take things too seriously, even when they are grave. The suffering of someone twisted in agony is just as tragic, but it is also just as impermanent!

Let us not add to suffering by indulging our attraction to tragedy, our tendency to exalt it and fix upon it. Let us not enter into other people's emotions, adding their pain to our own: "I suffer, as you suffer." Compassion means welcoming pain without identifying with it. The consideration of impermanence can help us to attain this serenity in the face of any suffering: this, too, will pass.

We must love others as ourselves, but we must also love ourselves as others: to care for others as if they were ourselves, and to care for ourselves as if we were another. Let us speak to our painful organs and to our sick cells with love, as if we were a cherished other. This is a good practice, which is used in some contemporary healing techniques. When we are caught up in suffering, we see no end; we have the impression that it will last forever. Yet no matter how long it lasts, pain is not eternal. It also has an end. "I am unhappy. This is a bad moment, but it will pass."

Consideration of impermanence can also make us less attached to our personal happiness, for it is just as impermanent. There is no need to be upset when it ends: it was to be expected. This also means that we do not take any pain too seriously, whether our own, or another's. However, this must not be confused with indifference. We are far from being indifferent, yet without a certain distance, offered by the teaching of impermanence, we risk getting carried away and drowned by suffering, whether our own or others'. Nothing is destined to last in a world of composite things, which must someday decompose. The universe itself is not destined to last, not even the solar system and the stars. Why be attached to it? Why indulge in the idolatry of transitory things?

In Biblical language it is not impermanence that is spoken of but the danger of idolatry. The essence of idolatry is to allow something whose existence is relative to usurp the place of the Absolute, or God. Happiness and pain are relative realities. As with impermanence, the relaxation, which results from this realization, makes us more effective. By letting go of our attachment to happiness, we become happier and more grateful for what we have. Whenever we consider the presence of a friend as something we are owed, we become unhappy (he didn't visit me, she didn't write to me, and so on). If, on the contrary, we consider that the other owes us nothing, we taste the instant more fully when they are able to be with us, or communicate with us.

The consideration of the impermanence of both happiness and unhappiness awaken a quality of compassion in us and an ability to be present with others' suffering. This person I am caring for will not always be in this state of suffering. Now is the time for me to perhaps do something to help them. When people talk about permanent schizophrenia, they are not in touch with the truth of impermanence. The painful pathology is a creation of time, and therefore impermanent. This does not prevent a person from living with this condition in a better way. The important thing is not to see beings as objects, not to label them by their behavior or attitude. We should beware of "diagnoses," which are merely labels in disguise!

In accompanying a dying person, it is important to remember that dying is a natural part of their mortal condition. We should not abandon them to their death, but allow them to leave in the best possible conditions. We should never offer false reassurances to them about their basic mortality. This is a lie, both to them and to ourselves. Some doctors give the impression that it is always wrong for their patients to die: as if death were not a natural part of life, a transition to be lived in the best way possible. When one accepts one's death, one can live the time remaining with far less pain.

Among the stages preceding death, as enumerated by Elisabeth Kübler-Ross, there comes a moment when one accepts the idea that one is going to die. Something in the body and in the psyche then lets go and stops suffering. There is an opening to the beyond and a cessation of identification with the psychophysical organism and its inevitable fate.

We are impermanent beings, we all share the same life of pain and happiness: we all belong to one vast family. Life is short, so why poison existence? Why create more suffering?

## BUDDHA-NATURE

There is a further Buddhist consideration that is of a higher level: the nature of Awakening is present as a seed in all being. In other words, "We all share the same Buddha-nature." Another way of saying this is that the Uncreated exists in the heart of all creatures. In the human there is also the divine.

We must go beyond the fear, aversion, and self-protection associated with the ordinary "me," which pollutes all our relation. If we develop this attitude of welcoming and opening, the other ceases to be a threatening stranger. We can see in them the Buddha-nature, the potential of awakening, and therefore as an aspect of the divine. "Whatever you do to even the least of my brothers, you do to me," said the Christ. This is why someone who has taken the way of compassion never loses sight of what is best and purest in other beings.

A good therapist looks not only at the disease, but also at what is healthy in the patient. The *Therapeutae* of Alexandria used the term "caring for Being." This may seem paradoxical, for it amounts to "caring for God." How can we "care for God" in another? What could that possibly mean? It means an approach where the cure begins with what is most wholesome in the other, with what has always been healthy. The Buddha-nature within us has never been sick, for it is already awake, unborn, unconditioned. We are already saved, cured, and healed, but we do not know it. We do not experience the salvation (*soteria*), which is the Holy Spirit within us.

It is not the physician who cures but nature. Any true therapist, of whatever sort, will place the patient in conditions, which allow nature to do its work. It is Being, which cures from the inside. This means that anyone who works for the welfare of all beings, whether in the role of a therapist or not, must realize that the well-being that is sought is already there. It is not something that must be brought in from the outside by a healer.

Whenever we care for someone we cannot remind ourselves too often that it is not we who are going to heal someone; we are simply going to create the inner and outer conditions, which are most favorable for the operation of what is already whole in that person. What is most precious does not need to be brought in by us, for it is already there, inside them. There is something unknown right in the middle of us; there is a dimension of life, fullness, and peace, which we have never tasted.

This consideration enables us to help others without despairing, for despair certainly lies in wait for us on this path. When we see all the terrible suffering in the world, it seems impossible to succeed. We must not lose faith that wholeness and happiness will ultimately have the last word. But such faith needs to be supported by some experience of awakening, or freedom (*soteria*) in ourselves.

This is why prayer is so important to all our acts. We call upon the Presence, the awakening of Spirit in the other, for it is only from the inside that they can be healed. When confronted with extremely difficult and painful mental illnesses, it is obvious that nothing can be done from the outside. In some forms of paranoia, for example, any outer action will only feed the delusory mechanism. But we can always call to the innermost Being of the person who is suffering, for that Being knows how to heal and save. Such a call, or prayer, is known as intercession.

If we are Buddhist, we see an individual as bearer of the Buddha-nature. It is possible to communicate with that nature, and therefore there is no need for fear. If we are Christian, we see the Christ within each individual. This reassures us and gives us true confidence that we may be able to help. Try to recognize with your heart the Christ within someone who is especially obnoxious, who is speaking to you in a repulsive way . . . and see what happens. It is surprising, and quite beneficial for both parties.

Hence we must keep in mind both the impermanence and interdependence in which we are all involved, whether we like it or not; and also the consideration that there is something in all of us that is free, unconditioned, and awake. This can help us to work for our own awakening and that of others. This attitude takes into account what is good for others and for ourselves. This is a win-win situation, where helping others is also helping oneself and vice versa.

Before wishing to save someone else, we must take care of ourselves as an integral part of the whole. We must take care of our body, this parcel of the material universe, which has been entrusted to us, but not as something separate and enclosed upon itself. That leads only to a dead end. When we care for another because they also belong to the whole of which we are a part, then the win-win situation manifests. Self-love and love for the other become one and the same love. There are not two loves. There is only love loving another and awakening to a dimension of happiness in this greater love.

We can love ourselves but not *for* ourselves. To love yourself for yourself is to block your capacity for happiness. To love yourself for others and for the world is the key to your happiness, and that of others as well. The ego, the mental structure in which we were enclosed, opens. True communication between yourself and the other begins to happen, and step-by-step, you discover the unity of all living beings.

We are endowed with a certain intelligence, which must be both cultivated and calmed. Have you ever noticed the difference between two types of meditation? In many respects they appear the same: the posture, the silence, the calm, and so forth. But inwardly, there is a vast difference, according to whether one meditates for one's own benefit, or whether there is an opening into the well-being of the whole universe. The quality of meditation is very different when we have chosen the way of compassion. Once we are truly on this way, we no longer meditate for ourselves, for this is seen as a subtle reinforcement of the ego-bubble. Even in the Zen tradition, which places such extreme emphasis on posture, we still find this vow to practice for the good of all beings.

But before entering into the posture and silence, even lay Buddhists take this vow: "Though sentient beings are uncountable, I vow to lead them all to enlightenment; though passions and sufferings are numberless, I vow to conquer them all; however numerous the dharmas (callings, duties), I vow to accomplish them all; however difficult the way of the Buddha toward enlightenment, I vow to follow it to the end." Clearly, this is no small vow! Yet even it can be captured by the ego. . . .

It bears repeating that this is not a vow to do good to others. How many times have we heard others, or been surprised to hear ourselves, subject someone to that cliché: "It's for your own good." WE know the unintentional (and intentional) harm that can result from those words. As Alice Miller points out in her books, the psychology of many a tyrant had its beginning in parents who subjected them to things "for their own good." In the way of compassion, there is no desire to help another against their will. One never imposes any sort of help; better yet, one "does good without willing to do good." Through vigilance, we always return to this attitude where nothing is imposed on another. One only has to be open to a quality of energy and being, which wishes happiness for another, but only in a form that is best for them.

**Question: Jesus Christ became very angry toward the money changers in the Temple. Moses also was angry at times. When is it the right time for anger? Are not the money changers of our time destroying the house of the Father? Is a bodhisattva ever angry?**

Before speaking of Christ, Moses, or a bodhisattva, let us observe our own angers, and see what provokes them. Children become angry when they don't get what they want, when others resist their will, or when things simply take longer than expected. There is irritation, and all these are examples of the anger of a "me." This type of anger is generally related to immaturity—one cannot tolerate things not going our way, or others wanting something different from what we want.

When faced with injustice, we may feel a different type of anger grow within us. We see another person abused and despised, there are basically two possibilities: to say and do nothing, not reacting; or to express oneself with force, with a tone that is much like anger. The former reaction has nothing to do with kindness and nonviolence, and everything to do with cowardice. Righteous anger is that of someone who is like a bodhisattva, or the Christ—it is not a personal anger, coming from an irritable "self" but the anger for the Self, of a Love that is being despised and humiliated.

To love someone does not always mean being nice to him or her. It can also mean shaking them up. It is my belief that the Christ's anger in the temple came from his love for all, including the money changers, who are not in their proper place, as well as those whose prayers they are disturbing. This space was also the place where Gentiles had the right to come pray. His anger thus reminds us that meditation and prayer were not reserved for a few elite but for all.

What is the real origin of my own anger? Is it the ego defending its territory, or is it something that has its source in the desire for the well-being of all? Even a bodhisattva can become angry in the face of an intolerable injustice, but this anger leaves no trace or disturbance afterwards. How different this is from our habitual anger! We ruminate endlessly about it afterwards, perhaps even creating ulcers or other physical effects.

**Question: In today's world, we should become angry, should we not?**

It is not a question of "should" or "should not." The essential thing is not to lie to oneself. In certain situations, manifesting anger is the right attitude; in others it is not the right thing to manifest because it will only add to the violence. In the first case, anger unblocks the conflict and causes another to become more conscious. In the latter, it only adds to the unconsciousness and inflames the conflict.

**Question: What is the relevance of what you say for the political dimension of human beings?**

I cannot answer this question in a general way. My teaching is that things are not good or bad in themselves. I have just said this even about anger, so how could I possibly say that this or that political policy is good or bad in itself? The just attitude is the one that is able to adjust itself! That is why I cannot speak of political attitudes in general.

It can be dangerous to speak in a doctrinaire way about the question of nonviolence. It encourages situations where nonviolence is a justification for cowardice. Some people use the language of nonviolence to spare themselves the challenge of acting with compassion, strength, and fairness. Compassion also includes force. To live this compassion demands great energy. Jesus said, "Blessed are the meek;" he didn't say "Blessed are the weak!"

As for the relation between this attitude of inner compassion, good-will, and political decisions, life always brings us situations to which we must adapt, and no one ever said it would be easy! What was a good policy at one time may become a bad policy at another time. The way of compassion is also one in which the intellect (which is always trying to generalize what should or should not be done) must always be ready to reexamine its assumptions when faced with a real situation.

**Question: If you found yourself in 1940, knowing what you know now, what would be your attitude toward Hitler?**

How can I say? Perhaps I might have killed him, or perhaps not. It is impossible to know this abstractly. It is easy with hindsight to say what should or should not have been done, but this is not a real situation, as it was for the people of that period.

What is important is to awaken in ourselves a quality of vigilance and presence in the moment we are living—this is the only way to dwell in a state of mind that is capable of just action. Another example is the ideas one receives in a training program for accompanying dying persons. However useful these may be, one must be prepared to let them go and adapt to the real situation of the person dying.

Another example: imagine that this very evening we are going to encounter someone who is a dangerous criminal. It is not enough to follow rules of compassion one has been trained in thinking, "I have compassion for you, so go ahead and do what you want." No! It might be better to think: "I have compassion for you, and I do not want you to become even worse than you are. There might be something I can do to prevent you from doing harm." Certainly there are people who must be forcibly rendered harmless. Sending someone to prison is not necessarily a bad thing. There even exist people whose actions are saying, in effect:

"Do something! Stop me, lock me up, because I am going to do a lot of violence and harm."

An act of compassion is indeed an act, but I would refrain from saying what it is, because there are only particular cases and situations. It is so easy to say "this is right" or "this is wrong," when it comes to serious situations such as abortion or euthanasia. The truth is that there are situations where such an action is harmful and destructive, and others where it avoids a still greater evil.

Ultimately, there are no generalities on this path, though generalities may help us toward a more lucid judgment. But the right action will always be the one that is adapted to a unique situation. This requires a harmony between what I really think and what is in my heart. Though my heart is disposed toward a quality of kindness, this is not separate from truth and justice. Love without justice becomes mere emotion, or sentimentality. It is not a creative love, which is capable of bringing about better conditions of life for all.

This is why we must try to invite an attitude where we do good without wanting to do good. We may even reach a point where we do good without knowing it! These moments are when we are at our best. What passes through us is something better than we are. It is not the limited "me," which "wants to do" good. It is a force of nature and energy, which fills and is transmitted by our gestures and actions.

When we claim to desire the liberation or happiness of all beings, we must qualify this with the reminder that we never have the right to impose on others what we judge to be happiness from our ego. We must be able to do good without imposing it, with respect for the other's freedom. Love *is* this respect!

We may find ourselves in a situation where we would like to care for, help, or love someone, yet they refuse it. Can we love someone against his or her will? I believe it is entirely possible, but there is no need for it to be visible, or known by them. Yet our habit is to always want people to know that we love them. Why? Because we want something in return.

Some may take the words of Buddha or Christ as a sermon or moral lesson. But I believe their real intention is for us to feel their words as inviting us to realities, which we must experience for ourselves. We have an ingrained tendency to hear teachings as commandments, as "thou shalt" and "thou shalt not." Yet if we examine the Hebrew word *mitzvot,* which is often translated as commandments, we see that it literally means "exercises" or practices, which are to be experienced and verified. Just the simple experience of wishing someone well with no knowledge of what is good for them, will make us happier.

In the way of compassion, never believe anything merely because someone tells you it is so. You must verify for yourself that it is right. This will help you to advance, to become better, and bring a little more peace into the world, making it a little more livable. The bodhisattva vow is an inner commitment, a vow to oneself, a certain way of considering other beings and their welfare before our own.

# ELEVEN

# THE THREE ATTITUDES

## *The King, the Ferryman, the Shepherd*

In Tibetan Buddhism, there are three types of bodhisattva symbolizing the king, the ferryman, and the shepherd.

The king symbolizes one who works for the good of all by saying: "I must begin by becoming master of myself. I must bring about peace in myself; only then can I help others." Though his goal begins with himself, he is still on the same path of awakening and well-being for all.

The ferryman symbolizes one who is on the path but in the company of others.

The shepherd symbolizes one who is primarily concerned with others from the beginning, putting them always first, refusing to experience an awakening that does not include everyone.

We each have all these three archetypes within us, though some may be stronger than others.

The Christ favored the image of the shepherd. A number of Christian saints, including Paul and Thérèse of Lisieux, return constantly to this theme: "I do not want knowledge of God, peace, or paradise, as long as there is a single being who has not entered into this peace and knowledge." This is characteristic of a highly awakened state of consciousness. As long as there is violence, loathing, and despair in a single being, then a part of my own being remains in despair and in suffering, and I cannot be completely happy.

If we are sometimes visited by feelings of sadness and despair during meditation, they are not necessarily our own. They may come to us because we have made ourselves available, permeable, and open to the suffering of the universe. True meditation is no guarantee of constant peace and bliss. After all the work we have done on ourselves, how can it be that we experience such moments of despair and loathing? It is because we are not just working on ourselves as separate bodies but on the body of the universe, which enables us to experience another's suffering as our own.

Nevertheless, we need not become fixated upon our own suffering, whatever its origin. We offer it up, thus participating in the well-being of the universe. When we experience an illness or depression not as our own but as the universe's, we are one with all beings who experience this kind of suffering. That may appear a bit grandiose in writing, but it is not at all the case in experience. This is the attitude of the ferryman, and sometimes we can find a special wisdom in the letting go of our personal history, our small suffering, which tends to submerge us.

A bodhisattva is someone who lives the spirit of this vow and cultivates the qualities that enable one to feel one's body as something infinitely vaster. To take the bodhisattva vow is to renounce one's own limits, one's own hell, and closure. It is to feel that within us there is something far greater than our usual selves and that the other is really within us.

This recalls one of the key passages of the Gospels: "Whoever wants to save his life shall lose it, and whoever loses his life for me shall find it." This is a general principle, which even applies to biology: paleontological evidence indicates that species that take no risks have a tendency to stagnate and stop evolving. One can also find this principle in business and finance, where money that does not circulate, accepting some risk, loses its value. The superiority of giving over preserving has its reflections in many domains.

This reflects a fundamental ontogenetic law of the transformation of being. If the grain of wheat does not "die" in the earth, it will remain isolated and static, and never become a plant that gives fruit. The acorn that seeks to preserve its life will never become an oak. Contrary to what one might think, those who avoid risk, who keep and hold rather than give, are actually destroying themselves. Only the death of the self can allow the Self to manifest in life.

The way of compassion requires a deep faith in this possibility. That is why one begins with faith in the Buddha-nature, in awakening, in the divine, or in the Christ-nature in us. This faith has its basis in these two understandings:

1. We must first understand how our existential pain is a consequence of the emotional struggles of our ego. The origin of all that does evil to us, and introduces disquiet into the world, is always because of the presence of ego, of some sort of "me," which advances itself at the expense of others.

   It is interesting to consider the economic implications of this. In his book *Reciprocity,* Serge-Christophe Kolm attempts to establish a link between these teachings and the current economy. He shows that an economy based on profit and the accumulation of wealth can only lead to a dead end: conflicts, wars, and the destruction of society. In political and economic terms, he expresses the Buddha's teaching that the source of suffering and disquiet, whether at the individual, social, or cosmic level, has its roots in the madness of the separate self, which seeks its own advantage at the expense of others. The bodhisattva attitude of desiring the well-being of others is a way of curing this disease in nature and in society. It represents the beginning of understanding.

2. The second element is an understanding that the Buddha-nature in each of us offers a possibility of liberation. If there were not already the unborn, unconstructed, and uncreated within us,

there would be no freedom for what is born, constructed, and created. If there were not already within us this space, freedom, and emptiness, we would be nothing more than beings whose destiny is death; and death would have the last word. Yet there is a way, which leads beyond this world destined for death, because within us there is something that is unconstructed and therefore cannot decompose, something that is uncreated, and therefore cannot die.

Meister Eckhart speaks of the uncreated as a dimension of human being and human history that does not belong to space-time. If this opening did not exist, we would be in hell, prisoners of the cycles of time, and of the law of cause and effect. We must understand and affirm this possibility of liberation as a way out of the prison. Otherwise, there would be no point in working for the welfare of all beings. In fact, total passivity would be the lesser of evils!

# TWELVE

# THE SIX PERFECTIONS, OR THE SIX PARAMITAS

How to escape these mechanisms of the ordinary ego: protection/defense, possessiveness/greed? How can we go beyond the ingrained attitude, which is always ready to grasp at what is judged as good and avoid what is judged as bad? The usual ego-based behavior is based on a closed-minded attitude. On the one hand, one is always seeking to protect and defend oneself, and on the other hand, one is always grasping, always wanting more.

"I call this good because it gives me pleasure; I call that bad because it gives me displeasure." This is the foundation of the egocentric attitude. In the Book of Genesis, it is symbolized by the fruit of the Tree of the Knowledge of Good and Evil, responsible for our downfall. The knowledge of that tree is an egocentric one: I see all things and events as they relate to my separate self, and I appoint myself judge of everything. Whatever I like or dislike is the criterion for what is judged as good or evil.

The Tree of Life, on the contrary, is a *theocentric* knowledge: I see all things, not as they relate to me but in their relation to Being, independent of my likes and dislikes. If Being has brought something about, it is not for me to judge whether it is good or evil.

In the Book of Genesis, we are given two choices: to live egocentrically, seeing things as they relate to us; or to live and to see things in relation to Being, allowing it to occupy the center of all, and to be what it is, whatever the conditioning linked to our memories and reactions. To live on the basis of "I like this, I don't like that," is to live in an attitude of fear. This fear originates in the ego, which constantly struggles to maintain and defend itself. It is astonishing how much energy is wasted in living constantly on the defensive. This fear leads us to close in upon ourselves, in an egoic cocoon that stifles us.

How can we get out of this?

First of all, we must believe that it is possible! Awakening this faith is not a given. Often people fall back into resignation and defeat: "I can never get out—suffering, violence, and stupidity will always win in the long run." Behind this act of courage, faith, and confidence, is a perception that the ego-based way of being is not the only possible one. We do not have to live in fear and self-protection, always wanting and seeking more. Another way of being is possible.

But it is realized only to the degree that we ground ourselves in the Buddha-nature, where one does not act from the separate self but from awakening, from the Christ, who is in us all. I see that "I" do not know how to love, that "I" can never truly love. But there is something far greater within me, which can love, and can act in a way with which I am not familiar. If I allow this Christ within me to express itself, I will be capable of things, which I could never accomplish through my separate self.

An example is the inability to forgive a certain offender. "I cannot forgive them. The more I try, the more hypocritical I become." It's true that there is no point in pretending otherwise and increasing the effort and hypocrisy. Some deeds are unforgivable, and we should not seek to forgive them with the force of our "me." Also it is an illusion to strain ourselves to become a better, more forgiving person, for we are simply not capable of this on the level of the ego. But the moment I truly recognize the limits of my love and my capacity to love and forgive, I can also open to "something" within me that is capable of loving. At this point we enter into contact with our true nature, which is unconditional generosity and kindness.

On the way of compassion, we discover that the ground of our being is goodness and that our deepest nature is to give. This is not obvious at first. Yet this fundamental generosity within us is very real and is known as the first of all the perfections.

In order to truly give in this way, however, we must overcome the beggar's conditioning, a deeply ingrained attitude, which makes us constantly in need of others and always wanting something from them. This attitude cannot see how it is possible to give without expecting something in return, and it is never really satisfied with what it does receive. Our parents never loved us "enough," and we are always fundamentally needy. As long as we remain in this beggar's conditioning, the fundamental generosity of our being is prevented from awakening. Thus we must get out of it.

Here are two Buddhist stories, which are often difficult for the Western mind to comprehend.

The first is that of a very poor woman who begged every day for her food. One day she heard that the Buddha was coming, so she was determined to meet him. When she got close enough to speak to him, she asked him for food.

"What do you really want?" the Buddha asked in return.

"I want some of those fruits you have in your bowl."

"I will give you some," the Buddha answered, "but first you must refuse what I am giving you."

Then he held out the fruits to her:

"Now—say 'No!'"

It was a very difficult thing for this starving woman, who could only feel one word, "Yes!" resounding in her, as she stared at the delicious fruits he was holding out. Nevertheless, she was silent, and allowed the "No!" to grow inside her.

At the instant she uttered the word, she realized that for her entire life, she had been begging inwardly as well as outwardly, which had made her dependent on others' gifts. In saying "No!" in this way for the first time, she also discovered that there was a strength in her that was capable of refusing a desire or an immediate need.

The Buddha then explained that we are all beggars, in the sense that we are always demanding things from life, never truly content. To the extent that we harbor this attitude, we overlook the treasure that is already within us. The Buddha's teaching does not say that we are poor and worthless; on the contrary, it declares that we are rich, even when we seem to have nothing.

"No matter how poor you are; you always have the capacity to give." This teaching is extremely important for the way of compassion. Whatever our outward wealth or poverty, including intellectual and other gifts, there is always within us this capacity to give, even if it is only our presence, our time, or our suffering. The essential nature of our being is this possibility of giving.

The second story comes from Tibet and is about two brothers who raise yaks. One of them was ambitious, always wanting more yaks, no matter how many he had. The other was always content with what he had, and at the moment he had only one yak. One day the two brothers met, and the one with the large herd said to the other:

"My dream has always been to possess a hundred yaks. But I only have ninety-nine. Could you please give me yours?"

"Of course," the other replied, "take it!"

When I first heard this story, I remember being a bit shocked by the injustice of it. The Tibetan lama who told it to me explained that the brother who was really poor was not the one left with no yaks but the one with many. Even with his hundred yaks, he would not be satisfied for long—he would always want more and more yaks, and would always be caught up in suffering. The wealthy brother was the one who was always living in the freedom and power to give. That is true wealth!

The true lord and master is one who is capable of giving. The lama continued: "As long as you have not lost your capacity to give, even if you have only a bit of breath to offer, even if you have only your presence to offer, you are a lord." At the moment of death, one offers up one's last breath. As it says in the Tibetan Book of the Dead: "Even my death, may it contribute to the welfare of all sentient beings." Nothing is ever lost when one is in this state of mind.

The state of mind most favorable for the awakening of oneself and of others is that in which one returns to the capacity to give, to the generosity that is our true nature. No matter how much poverty we experience, we can always give. For some of us, this is a difficult message to hear because we are so conditioned to demand and accumulate.

The story of the two brothers teaches us that the more we need, desire, and accumulate, the more unhappy and dissatisfied we become. On the contrary, the less we possess and accumulate, the freer we are. We have the power to let go of things. The way of liberation on this path is not to accumulate more, so as to become rich but to give more, so as to become rich. The only thing that can never be taken from us is what we give. This is simple in theory. But can we really live this way?

The Gospels teach "There is more joy in giving than in receiving. To him who gives, it shall be given." In contrast, there is a strange saying of Jesus, which seems to contradict this: "He who has, to him shall be given; and he who has not, from him shall be taken even the little that he has." What this means is this: to those who have charity, the capacity to give, openness of the heart, everything shall be given. But to those who have not this capacity, everything shall be taken away because they have lost the gift.

**Question: Does it not flatter our ego to give to others?**
There are different ways of giving. Obviously, it is possible to give ostentatiously, so as to be well considered, with one's name prominently displayed, perhaps even having a charity named after the donor, so that future generations will remember, and so on. Another way of giving is in order to receive affection from another. The more we shower them with gifts, the more they will shower us with love!

There are also different qualities of gift: material, emotional, or spiritual. When the Buddha asked the hungry woman what she really wanted, it was similar to the Christ, who said to the Samaritan woman: "Whoever drinks this water will be thirsty again."

Once when I was in India, walking with a young swami in the streets of Bombay, we passed a woman who seemed to be in very bad shape, and in need of help in crossing the street.

"Let's help her," I said spontaneously.

"No, no!" the swami replied. "You will only prevent her from living out her karma. If she is in a bad state, it is because she has done bad things in this life, or in past lives. You Westerners are too sentimental. Helping her will do no good, and you will simply comfort her ego, which will do her harm. She must get out of this by her own efforts, that is the only way she will attain liberation."

"Well, I know one thing," I replied. "If I don't help her, it will be bad karma for me. I'm not asking you to participate, but I'm going to help her. If I don't, it will bother me for the rest of the day. You may see this as comforting my ego as well as hers. But I don't see how help given in this attitude can possibly be an obstacle to awakening!"

We must not have fear of giving, yet at the same time, we must beware of excess in our "giving." An example is the danger of spoiling or overprotecting children, which prevents them from finding their own way, and from asking authentic questions. Again, the question is not some generality about whether it is good or bad to give. In one situation, it may be right to give a lot, whereas that amount would be far too much—or too little—in other situations.

The important thing is to have the discrimination necessary to confront concrete situations. By wanting to give too much, one can sometimes do real harm, stifling and even killing a person's individuality. Unintelligent love can crush a person and prevent them from breathing.

Sometimes we think we have given a lot, but what we gave was not what the other really needed. This brings us back to the necessity of discrimination. When we are solidly grounded in our capacity to give, we do not need to give compulsively, especially when there is no real call to do so.

Within us is the gift, which is the capacity to give. Many people suffer from not being able to give their love. It is a terrible pain to feel the treasures of generosity and compassion within us, and yet have no one to receive them, no one who wants them. Untransmitted love can ultimately destroy us.

What can we do with this energy, which can harm us or even destroy us, if we do not "spend" it? Here is where the process of inner transformation through prayer and meditation can help. Through this practice, the energy is not lost but offered up. Through prayer and meditation one can indeed transmit and channel this energy for the well-being of all creatures. It does not have to be transmitted to a specific being. This principle operates like a physical law. We do not really know where the energy goes or who benefits from it. We do not know what will be the effects of this loving kindness that fills us, taking the form of a prayer, which asks for the welfare of all beings. We are centered in a generosity that is totally disinterested.

The way of compassion reminds us that we are not beggars, no matter how dire our poverty, no matter what our unmet needs, no matter how terrible our parents were, no matter what our failures in "obtaining" love. We are still rich to the extent that we are in touch with our gift of giving. This is our true nobility. Some Buddhists translate bodhisattva as "noble being."

This is why fabulously wealthy people are totally lacking in nobility. They have everything, they have far too much, and yet they are in a permanent state of need. Obsessed by their possessions, these people have lost the simple ability to let go, and this is true misery. Others, who may possess very little, can be astonishing in their generosity. They offer things readily, not even thinking of themselves as generous because it is so natural to share what you have.

The nobility of those who are on the path of awakening and compassion originates in the Being within them, which is capable of giving.

Through the exercise of this gift, they are grounded in their essential nature, the living Christ within. To be grounded in our essential nature is to be grounded in our essential nobility. In his first Epistle, St. John says: "He who does not love dwells in death. He who loves dwells in God, and God in him." These simple words tell us that the very act of loving, of expressing this generosity within us, is none other than God, living within us and through us.

In the story of the two brothers, another possible objection is that the brother who gave up his last yak was not doing any sort of real good for anyone. However, this forgets that he was at least doing good to himself, being faithful to the Life and the Divine within him. Yet it is true that the other brother received no benefit, because he remained trapped in greed and dissatisfaction. He was incapable of doing good to others and quite ready to take away their last possessions.

What I would like to do is to convince you without trying to convince you! The story of the two brothers helps us to understand this, for we have both brothers within us and sometimes vacillate between them. There are days when we are possessed by the craving for more, and other days when we could give away everything we possess. Yet even if we gave away all our possessions or were stripped of them, we would still have the ability to give, which no one can ever take away from us.

"Blessed are those of goodwill! Peace to those of goodwill!" Goodwill, or loving kindness, is desire that is oriented toward the good. It is not enough, but this is where we must begin. If we cultivate this will to do good and to discover reality within us, I believe we have nothing to fear. The vicissitudes and dilemmas of life will not stop us; there will always come a time when we get back on the path.

When the desire for awakening, freedom, peace of mind, and intelligence takes deep root within us (for all beings, not just for ourselves), it will save us from all sorts of unhealthy attachments, dead ends, and traps of suffering. We will cease to be possessed by what we possess. This desire is what maintains vigilance and openness of the heart.

Now let us speak of practice.

The bodhicitta of practice means an attitude of awakening within one's practice. This consists of developing the six perfections; in other words, the perfection of these six qualities. "I have not come to abolish the law but to fulfill it," Jesus said. We have also come to fulfill, to go all the way in realizing what has already been given to us. To recall the six perfections: giving; discipline, patience; energy; meditation; and finally—wisdom—which is also called transcendent knowledge.

There is a kind of scale or hierarchy involved here. It is a totally practical way, based on accomplishing one step after another, always starting from where you are.

We must remember that before we can hope to love humanity or love our enemies, we must first love our whole body, from our breath to our feet. In the beginning, there is love within us but we do not know how to love. We can at least love a plant, a dog, our breath, our life. Sometimes it is difficult to love life—yet if we do not love life, love to be alive, how can we possibly be of any use or help to others?

Before loving the life of another perhaps we should first love this most intimate place where life passes: ourselves. Then we can say: "I do nothing, but I love life! I love the life that animates me. And from this faithful affection and loving kindness toward the life that breathes me, perhaps this love can be communicated further . . ."

The quality of giving is the first one to be developed.

# THIRTEEN

# GIVING

This brings us to practice. The foundation of being is sheer generosity, which is manifested in the simple fact of the existence of the universe, and we must live in this current. This implies uniting with the creative energy in us, for not to love is to move away from life and ultimately to dwell in death.

We shall examine and distinguish different concrete forms of giving: the gift of material things; the gift of protection; the gift of love; the gift of loving-kindness; and finally, the gift of *Dharma,* which means the gift of truth. This practice begins with concrete giving, in an attitude of well-wishing and availability.

How can this become incarnate, and take form in us?

## THE GIFT OF MATERIAL THINGS

In all the great religions, great importance is given to material charity, not for its quantity but for its quality of giving. In the Gospels, we find the parable of the widow who has only a few coins, yet puts them all in the collection box of the temple. Jesus says that this woman has given far more than all the others, because she gave even what she needed. This is also a recurrent theme in the Pali scriptures: it is the quality, not the quantity, of the gift that is important. A true gift is from the heart.

There are several types of gift of material things from one who has, to one who has not, or to who is in need. One gives material things to monks, for example, and in return, they are expected to make spiritual gifts, such as teaching, helpful words, or a prayer, which helps others to evolve or awaken. Without entering into further details we note that kind of exchange has been established since ancient times and exists in many traditions.

Whoever wishes to receive inner gifts must make outer gifts: this is the founding principle of charity to monks. It is not unlike the custom of offering a fruit or flower to a teacher. The gesture itself helps to open the giver inwardly, making them more able to receive the teaching.

Giving material things to those who ask, or for social causes, are expressed through very specific acts. This is a very good occasion to practice self-observation! To what degree are we attached? Are we identifying ourselves with something, finding security in it, and therefore according value to things that are superficial, short-lived, and lacking in true worth?

All these practices offer an occasion to help us break free of the old ego-habits, which always seek security and protection, and breed fear of letting go. Opening our attitude with regard to our possessions can be an incomparable aid to opening the heart. When you give to someone it may not necessarily be because they really deserve it—you cannot always know whether it is the right thing for them or not—but you can know whether it is the right thing for you. It is right when it reopens you to your fundamental nature, enlivening you with the current of its generosity.

Of course we must exercise discrimination. It is not good to give in all circumstances—for example, when you know that someone is begging money to buy drugs. Nevertheless, you can still give, even in this situation. You can at least give your kindness, and your recognition of them, which may even give them a bit more awareness in their life. There are times when merely giving money is actually a way of avoiding true giving of ourselves. The money acts as a substitute for the gift of our true presence.

## THE GIFT OF PROTECTION

One can also offer protection. The way of compassion teaches us that it is not the desire to give something that is crucial, but being open and not closing ourselves to the needs of others. For someone who needs protection we can at least offer them the asylum of our goodwill and prayer.

Sometimes people may need reassurance or consolation. It is a form of protection to be able to offer them our presence through the right gesture, or perhaps affection—yet avoiding an attitude, which labels them in their need. May our gift to them always include the capacity to free them from needing us! A good father should give his children the protection they need but also the ability to be independent of him, to produce something on their own. This is not easy.

The gift of protection must not degenerate into protectionism, or paternalism. True aid to developing countries is not necessarily giving them things but helping them to get along without us! Otherwise, rich and poor countries are caught in a vicious circle of dependence, where rich countries mask their guilt by dumping their surplus wealth.

## THE GIFT OF LOVE

More than protection, we need love. Bodhisattva figures often have symbolically open arms—yet they never embrace anyone. This may seem odd, but what it means is that they are open to others; yet they never close them in with their love. Bodhisattvas do not love others because of any benefit to themselves. How to love another without holding him or her for oneself is a psychologically complex question. The other may in fact want you to be possessive, because they mistake that as a sign of love. This can create very difficult knots in relationships.

How to really love someone? By expressing words, deeds, and feelings, which make them feel loved but not locked inside in your arms, in a possessive affection in which they cannot be free. This is a love, which can say: "I love you but not to keep you for myself. Follow your true way, do not worry about me, do not become dependent on me."

This recalls the frequent comments of Karlfried Graf Dürkheim regarding spiritual teachers. They should be like fuel pumps, which help one to continue one's voyage. It would make no sense to hang around the fuel pump interminably after it is full, yet that is what people do with spiritual teachers. When the tank is full they encourage the traveler to continue his or her own voyage.

Compassionate love, which is not a love of passionate attachment, is close to the attitude of the true psychotherapist. These therapists must accept the phenomenon of positive transference, realizing that the love of the patient is not really for them but for an image, which the patient needs temporarily, in order to break through and go further. The therapist never rejects the transference. It must be accepted, but like the bodhisattva, in a spirit of open arms, which never close upon the patient. Then they can find a way to tell the patient: "It is not me whom you love; you are looking for something else. I am only a face that you love. Do not confuse what you love with me. It will only create attachment, then difficulties, then alienation."

This is encountered even in ordinary couple-relationships: I fall in love with an image of the other, and the other with an image of me. With maturity, we will both realize that we must go beyond images and begin to love the other for himself or herself. Then we are both free. But there can be no letting go unless there is first an embrace. Some people want to take a shortcut, and let go from the start. This is a misunderstanding of the teaching of nonattachment. The doctrine of the illusory nature of separate beings becomes a pretext for a kind of indifference to them. Even illusory, impermanent beings have a need to be held in someone's arms. It is not the arms holding them that is the problem, it is when the arms become locked, so that when the time for letting go of the image has come, there can be no opening.

The practice of giving and the way of compassion in a love relationship is one of the most difficult challenges of life. We must not be caught in either of two extremes: sentimental love and emotional attachment on the one hand, or dryness, distance, and indifference, on the other hand. We must find the middle way, which at times is like a razor's edge.

Our purpose on Earth is to learn to love truly. To love is not so difficult but to love truly . . . what a path! It is my belief that we spend our entire lives learning this. We need time in order to see how we were really not loving well, how we were self-centered in our love. We desire all sorts of gross and subtle rewards, and we call that love . . .

**Question: What is the proper place of passionate love?**

In compassion, there is no place for love that is dependent on passion. We can allow a passion to develop, based on our image of someone, and still dwell in the knowledge that this is not Being and is not true Existence. Love and knowledge are in reality inseparable. To offer infinite love to someone or something that is not the Infinite is to be in ignorance and suffering.

True love is a kind of wisdom. To love someone for whom they are, but not in inappropriate excess, is true love. What we often call passion is a projection of the infinite onto the finite. Suddenly, this being becomes a surrogate for our infinite. He or she becomes "everything" for us. But a living being is a part of the Whole—and they are a being infinitely loveable as such—but they are not the Whole itself, they are not the totality of God.

It is true that the practice of meditation, which brings about awareness of the impermanence of the "me" of our thoughts and emotions, renders us less susceptible to the onslaught of passion. In fact, we see that the desire to make another into a kind of All or Absolute is really a form of lying to ourselves. It is based on ignorance. But most of us are so conditioned to respect this kind of passion that it is actually startling to meet someone like the Dalai Lama, whose tangible radiance of love and compassion is so universal and transpersonal.

When I was living in New York, the Dalai Lama was invited to the university where I was teaching.

After he had passed among us, a colleague spoke to me. "Did you notice how he looked at me?" she said.

"Yes, I noticed how he looked at you," I replied.

The visit continued for a while, and at one point the Dalai Lama, who is known to be very interested in machines, stopped to look at one.

"Did you notice how he looked at that machine?" I asked her.

Both looks were very much the same. Of course one does not look at a person the same way one looks at a machine. But the quality of attention and openness was the same. In this context, love is not so much a relationship as it is a state of being, a state of consciousness, and loving-kindness. It is true that this kind of love lacks that person-to-person exclusivity we are so fascinated with in our Western stories of love, with their beauty and tragedy: "There is no you but you, my one and only!"

On the way of compassion, it is not relationships we seek to develop but a capacity of loving kindness toward all beings, no matter who or what they are. Of course we can also accord a special privilege to certain relationships—thank God!—but a relationship derives its privilege from a conscious accord of minds.

In the Gospels, the question arises as to the identity of the disciple "whom Jesus loved." Could it be that Jesus loved John more than, say, Peter? No. Jesus loved Peter as much as he did John, and even Judas, for he was the incarnation of love. The sun shines alike on the good and the bad, the just and the unjust, as he himself said. There is just as much love available for Judas as there is for John. But this does not mean Jesus did not have a special affinity with John. It is not "more love" but a kind of resonance and mutual understanding that makes a relationship privileged.

The quality of giving, which must be awakened in us, is a state of consciousness that remains steadfast in all circumstances. When there is no longer anyone who loves us, when the marvelous man or woman one has been so attached to is gone—either because they have died, or left us for another—how do we maintain this quality of love, which we experienced in their presence? This is a crucial question.

On the way of compassion, it is right and proper to make use of a special beloved face or image but only so as to awaken a quality of love within us, which is independent of that face or image. Otherwise, when they are gone, it will be as if our love has gone with them. To identify love with the person who awakened it within us is a melodrama common in the West. But the quality of love can continue quite well when the person is gone. I can even give this love to a blade of grass, to the wind, to all beings. For all of them are the face of the Beloved.

## THE GIFT OF LOVING-KINDNESS

Loving-kindness, or goodwill—"the sun, which shines on the just and the unjust"—is the Good itself, which radiates itself, no matter what the subject or object toward which it turns.

## THE GIFT OF TRUTH

Finally, we come to what is called the "Dharma" in Buddhist language, which means the Teaching or the Truth. The Buddha considered this to be the greatest gift: to teach someone how to see what is true. We also find this teaching in Christianity. "The highest charity is the gift of truth," according to Thomas Aquinas.

Loving someone and being truthful to them are inseparable. One must have great love for another in order to communicate truth to them. Telling the truth can arouse fear: "She will stop loving me if I tell her what I really think." But the *manner* in which one communicates truth is crucial, and this is where we find the link between wisdom and love. A truth told with a tone of condescension or violence will be destructive. Yet that same truth told with love can be liberating.

Often, we must "shake up" someone with one hand (the hand of rigor), while caressing them with the other (the hand of kindness). In many icons of the Christ, we can observe that one eye is soft, and the other hard. In the eye of kindness and mercy, we accept the other as they are. The other eye demands discrimination, and justice. Together, they offer love without indulgence.

It seems to me that this corresponds to the dual need in us: to be loved as we are; and to be told the truth about how we are. To tell us comforting fables will only add to the illusion, which is an obstacle to our freedom. The greatest gift we can give to others is that of the truth, which helps them on the path to awakening. To work for the welfare of all living beings is to want them to live in awakening and knowledge.

### A MOMENT OF MEDITATION

*Let us experience this moment of meditation as a gift. Let us give our time, our body, our mind, our attention, and our breath. To whom?*

*We might offer it to a particular person, someone who is dear to us, or who is in need of our meditation and prayer. To direct this energy through the thought of the heart, toward this person, can be both a help and a support. Let us offer this moment of time, this breathing, this moment that is given us, to that person's well-being.*

*One can also offer this energy up to Breath, to Life. Let us invite the Living One in us to bless all that exists, welcoming everything into our heart and mind—the world as it is, with all its sufferings and questions. All is within us, so let us breathe deeply, with kindness, with universal friendliness and lucidity, for our well-being, and the well-being of all.*

# FOURTEEN

# DISCIPLINE

This is known as the second *paramita,* the second perfection. How can discipline be reconciled with freedom? It often seems that discipline is the enemy of freedom. Yet no one is forcing us to choose this discipline. It is related to taking a vow. "Why did I do that? Because I vowed to do it. Because I find that this vow favors the attitude, which is most open, most just, and the least closed-minded. Because it offers me more access to the very experience of the Living One."

The decision to accept discipline is a free one. It is a skillful means of returning to one's true Self. It is a means of working on the obstacles, difficulties, and pathologies of the self, so as to render it more available to the Self. It favors the wakefulness that is our essential nature. A discipline normally also proposes certain exercises and acts of observation. The primordial exercise, however, is to pay attention, in every moment, to our reactions: to see how great is our tendency to get caught in the trap of reactivity.

Traditionally, this discipline is codified in what is called the ten negative and the ten positive actions. The most important thing is to observe the negative actions of the body, the negative actions of the mind, and the negative actions of speech.

# FIFTEEN

# THREE NEGATIVE
# ACTIONS OF THE BODY

I t is not enough to take a vow to save all beings, to have an immense heart, to be open to all, or to be unafraid of suffering. Practice is necessary. It begins where we are, and where we are is in egocentrism, with habits of behavior that are more or less in error because they prevent us from tasting the depths of our being.

## KILLING

The first negative physical act is that of killing, or more exactly, taking life, arrogating life. Killing is usually an act, which is either based on some form of attachment—seizing something or someone for oneself—or on aggression. The goal of spiritual teaching is to help us live in an attitude of nonattachment and nonaggression. It is also an attitude of harmlessness, of respect for life in all its forms, whether human, animal, or plant.

A bodhisattva avoids taking life in any form. Not to kill, not to destroy, is to act from an attitude of respect for all existence. This also implies attention toward one's own acts and behavior. Many people raise the question of food. We find ourselves in a world where the continuation of life depends on the death of other forms of life. This applies to animals also, whether or not we eat their flesh.

According to one story, the Buddha died from food poisoning from bad pork. Normally, he did not eat such food, but he was invited to eat by a woman who had only a bit of stew to offer him, and he kindly accepted. This fearless, compassionate acceptance led to his death. Clearly, the Buddha was not obsessed by food, as some interpretations would have it. This story shows that compassion was for him a higher value than perfection in not killing.

Tibetan lamas eat meat. The Dalai Lama has often pointed out that the important thing is to receive food as a gift from the animal or the person who offers it to us. To accept it as a gift returns it to the flow of life. This is an attitude of openness, which adapts to circumstances and avoids dogmatism.

Kalu Rinpoche, on the other hand, would buy live fish in markets, so as to throw them back into the sea. It was his rather theatrical way of showing the importance of respect for all life. In Christianity, we have much to learn from this. We tend to be too anthropocentric, so concerned with human life that we forget that it depends on other forms of life and on the environment.

What we can do is to kill less and less and transform death through an offering, through consecration and recognition of the gift. To receive a meal is to receive an offering, a gift, a sacrifice of another form of life. All being gives itself to other being. In a number of Buddhist stories, animals voluntarily offer themselves to humans who are hungry. Our gratitude must also include plants and all elements that nourish us, giving themselves to us and to our growth.

These forms of life are given us, and in return we must give ourselves. This is essential to the circulation and reproduction of life. Each time we are given something, we should somehow give in return. If we do not, the gift will stagnate in us, and finally make us sick and unhappy. Much suffering and illness originate in this kind of blockage of the potential to love and give. We may search endlessly for objects "worthy" of our love, but everything is worthy of our love. If we are somehow prevented from loving the person to whom we are most attracted, we can still love other persons. The face of Life has many forms, not necessarily like the ones that we identify as such. We think we know how to recognize Life and overlook it when it is right in front of us.

This reminds me of a Christian story of a spiritual teacher, who had promised to visit the house of his disciple on Christmas day. The man was busy preparing his house to receive the master. A homeless woman knocked at the door and asked for shelter. He refused, saying that he could not welcome her on this day, because he was preparing the house to receive the great man.

The master arrived as the woman was leaving, and said:

"That woman who asked you for shelter was me."

The capacity for giving and hospitality within us is meant to be expressed. As Jesus said, when we have given our whole life, then it can never be taken from us. Bodhisattvas and saints are fearless in the face of death, because they have already given their lives. In contrast to this, we grasp and cling to life. When you accompany dying people, you see how some of them cling to what was not made to last, right up to the last moment, whereas others give themselves, and continue giving with their last breath. "He rendered his spirit," it is said of Jesus when he died. Yet the literal translation of *spiritus, pneuma,* or *ruakh,* is "breath," which means that he transmitted, or gave, his Breath.

At the moment of death, certain people are still able to give. If you are lucky enough to receive this gift, you will see that it is tremendous, for they have transmitted it to you in a very real way. Such transmissions take many traditional forms: from parent to child, from teacher to disciples, and so forth.

On the way of compassion, we are always reminded that everything we possess will be taken from us, so that in giving and sharing it, we free ourselves of a certain rigidity. This enables us to savor that which can never be taken from us.

## TAKING WHAT IS NOT OURS (THEFT)

Because of attachment or aggression, we may be tempted to take what does not belong to us, through the use of force or stealth. There are some who preach that all of our excess possessions are the result of theft from those who are in need. Why do we accumulate things? Because we are afraid, because we are haunted by a sense of insecurity. This always has its origin in the ego, which identifies with its wealth and possessions.

To engage ourselves in the way of compassion is to lighten up, to empty our closets and attics a bit, to invite more space into our lives. How much better this can make us feel! Yet this should never be taken as a commandment or ethical rule. No one has the right to tell you to empty out your closets or that it is wrong for you to have too many things. This is not an eternal moral law but an invitation to each individual to sense this stifling feeling within them, which results from too little space. In this sense, there is a more subtle theft, which is to accumulate things we don't need and could be useful to others.

At a certain point this becomes obvious. But first, there must be an opening of the heart to the Self; otherwise, it will just be a trick of the ego, which now wants to be outwardly poor so as to be seen as more spiritual. An authentic act of generosity flows directly from the source, and we have no concern for whether or not others are aware of it. Their happiness is a part of our own well-being.

## MISUSE OF SEXUALITY

In itself, sexuality is good, for it is a natural element of the human creature. It is part of the gift of the energy within us and is the desire to give and receive but only as a relation between two subjects. It is misused when it violates the attitude of compassion, which requires that we never treat another as an object.

By sexuality, I do not necessarily mean genital sex. Sexuality is inherent in the phenomenon of gender, in being masculine or feminine. There is a masculine way of giving oneself and a feminine way. This can express itself in forms independent of biological sexuality.

When any form of sexuality is used in a destructive or compulsive way, it reinforces the ego. We use others so as to dominate, manipulate, or possess them instead of experiencing a relationship of true sharing and exchange. Possessiveness can manifest in many kinds of situations. Sometimes it is identified with the sexual act: "This person belongs only to me!" Undoubtedly, there is a link between territoriality and sexuality. This is why bodhisattvas often avoid sexual relationships, sensing beforehand the emotions of possession and attachment, which they are bound to stir up. This does not imply a rejection of sexuality, however, but a rechanneling of it.

# SIXTEEN

# THREE POSITIVE ACTIONS
# OF THE BODY

M urder, theft, and the misuse of sexuality are three examples of negative physical actions. But there are also positive actions, which increase (instead of decrease) our access to our essential nature. We have already spoken of many of these.

Good physicians do not indulge in despair when confronted with disease, nor do they marvel at good health. Instead they look upon disease while remembering good health. Many doctors do not realize that illness is sometimes a means of curing oneself of a more profound disease.

The way of compassion asks us to observe our habits of appropriating things, of seeing other people, of gross and subtle ways of destroying, with our own style of theft or possessiveness. To observe this in everyday life is a powerful aid in the evolution of our attitudes and of our freedom with regard to them. We simply observe the negative aspects of our being, while remembering the positive aspects. These are traditionally classed as: protecting, giving, and good use of sexuality.

## PROTECTION

As an antidote to killing, the first positive act is to protect life in all its forms: human, animal, or plant. It also means participating as fully as possible in the cycles of nature and respecting them. Note that in this attitude, an ecological dimension is implicit. For a bodhisattva, caring for all beings naturally means caring for nature, including plants, animals, and humans (an animal species sick from an overdose of thought).

Anyone who knows how to truly care for plants or animals will also know how to care for human beings, for they will already have learned not to regard even "their" animals with possessiveness. Unfortunately, many people do the opposite and lavish excessive affection on an animal, while their human relations suffer as well. They cannot see that their neighbors could benefit from some of that affection. They have become objects, and so has the pet, whose animal nature suffers from lack of recognition and respect. Animals, like humans, need space in relationships.

## GIVING

The second positive action is the reverse of the second negative one: not only must we refrain from taking what is not ours; we must learn to give so as to participate in the generosity of the divine.

## GOOD USE OF SEXUALITY (CHASTITY)

In its original meaning, chastity is not an avoidance or a repression of sexuality. It means using sexuality with an unselfish attitude, which is grounded in love, intelligence, insight, and virtue.

In the Christian tradition, this has often come to mean abstention, but chastity is something far more subtle and interesting. It can be defined as refraining from ever treating the other as an object. We consume objects, we consume nature, and in consuming them we destroy them. In the same way, we consume each other. To be chaste is to remember that we never touch a "body;" we touch a person! We make love with a being, not with an object of pleasure. Hence we must free ourselves of the attitude of being consumers. Instead of a "consummation," sexuality can become a communion. Chastity makes communion possible.

"He who looks at a woman with lust has already committed adultery in his heart," as Jesus said in the Gospels. Many have objected to this dictum, but let us see what it really means. To look at a woman with lust is to stop seeing her as a real woman but as an object. It overlooks her as a person and blocks the possibility of a human relationship. This is unfortunate, because it is equivalent to overlooking reality itself.

The word *sin* originally means missing the mark, not seeing what is, missing being as it is. We must transform the way we look, ceasing to appropriate others, which reduces them to objects of consumption.

Even spirituality can become an object of consumption—the consumer-attitude knows no limits! Chastity is an attitude of love and respect before the mystery of Being, the sense of a Subject, which can never be comprehended as an object.

Chastity is also possible with regard to all things in the universe. It means renouncing the craving to *penetrate* their secret. There is a lack of chastity in a certain scientific attitude, which reduces living beings to objects, in an effort to penetrate their secret. A virtuous science seeks to understand the mysteries of the universe through the insight that knowledge is not something to be seized by us but to be revealed to us. There are many examples of scientists achieving the knowledge they have been seeking, but only when they finally relax their will to understand and allow things to be revealed as they are.

There is also a lack of chastity, which is often encountered among analytic psychotherapists. I am not referring to anything deriving from genitality here but to a frame of mind. Descriptions of a person as having paranoid behavior or being trapped in a schizophrenic system may have truth, but it is never the whole truth about that person! Here, the lack of chastity manifests as labeling another, thereby reducing them to a case, which is a form of object.

Whatever medical or psychological school one subscribes to, the practitioner can still respect the mystery of being in the patient before them, a being, which contains a secret that will always elude them. Respect for this mystery can also be expressed as respect for the patient's "divine nature"—in other words, something that always escapes our attempt to grasp it and make it an object of knowledge.

A true therapist in this sense, is capable of saying, in effect: "I can inform you of a number of facts about yourself, but these facts are not who you are. Who you are is infinitely more than I can understand. Using what I understand about your illness and your suffering, I will try to make you better. But there will always be something in you that escapes me."

When we speak of chastity in relation to "libido," we are not only speaking of the genital level. At any level, we must be vigilant so as to prevent relationships from deteriorating, always recalling that this other is a person like ourselves. This attitude of chastity can go much further, both in our relation to people and to material objects. Chastity is a form of knowledge, which respects the mystery of otherness that is in everything.

## A New Question Regarding Desire

There is a question as to the legitimacy of desire. But first we must be clear as to what this means. What we are speaking of is the possibility of a *disoriented* desire. Desire is disoriented to the extent that it tends toward possessiveness, objectification, and fixation. Wrong orientation of desire lies in its fixation upon an object, which overlooks the subject. It is a certain fixated way of looking, which transforms living water into a block of ice.

You may reply that desire itself is the flow of life within us, and this is quite true. But one can enjoy a flower without picking it. A proper orientation of desire does not consist in trying to stop this flow; on the contrary, it consists in *not* trying to stop it. It is normal and healthy to experience a flow of desire toward an attractive woman or man. But the subsequent craving to enclose them within this desire can lead to physical and psychological dependence and suffering.

It is fascinating to observe, on a concrete level, how our relationships can change when they are informed by an attitude of openness and a more fluid desire, which has no fixed aim. Love begins to manifest, not only during a particular moment, but also in all moments, and in our every gesture.

In an intimate relationship, as soon as one person gives in to the thought of "what is supposed to happen," the poison begins to operate and spread. Why do we so often speak of "preliminaries" in love-relationships, as if there were a precise goal to be attained? In this case, desire becomes obsessive to some degree, more or less fixed upon some outcome or another. On the other hand, if fluidity of desire is allowed to manifest fully, things happen in a different way. When pleasure arrives, it is like a blessing upon the desire, a kind of exultation in the event of this meeting. Far from being a problem, it makes the meeting all the more grand, wholesome, and holy. In fact, the less obsession, the deeper the pleasure, and it is experienced not as a goal that has been attained but as an unexpected gift.

"Seek the Kingdom first, and all the rest shall be added," in the words of the Gospels. If your primary concern is to love, to give, to live in the reign of spirit, then all else shall be given you, gratuitously, as a gift. But if you first seek pleasure, peace, and light for your own sake . . . you will likely miss them.

**Question: Are you not playing with words when you speak of pleasure? In the real world we live in, pleasure comes from seduction, does it not? We also want to be the object of another's desire, right? Isn't the pleasure of which you speak really a kind of nonpleasure?**
There are different styles and levels of pleasure. Of course there is the pleasure of the separate self, with its need for recognition. This ego thrives on seduction, but its type of pleasure is constantly under threat. There will always be people who are not attracted to you, and there is

bound to come a time—whether from fatigue, illness, or age—when your power of seduction fades. For those who know only this level of pleasure, growing old is a dreadful drama. They stand to lose their power of seduction, upon which their entire sense of identity is built. Only then do they begin to see that their narcissistic image is an illusion.

But we have the capacity to awaken to a state of consciousness and being where pleasure is no longer dependent on this ego. I would not describe it as any sort of nonpleasure but a different pleasure, a different quality of relationship. The old "I" has tremendous difficulty in accepting and understanding this pleasure. Nevertheless, there are certain privileged moments in our existence when we are given a taste of this other pleasure, and the ability to appreciate it, and to understand that the old pleasures, the ones to which we are often most attached, are not the only ones.

Sometimes we must undergo hardships, breakups, and narcissistic wounds, which shatter the flattering image that we had of ourselves, in order to discover two truths: that we are not who we thought we were; and that the loss of a cherished pleasure is not necessarily the loss of true happiness and well-being.

**Question: How is it possible to accept a transcendent reality? One can be agnostic in this regard, even though one is not an atheist.**
We must be clear about how we are using words: when you say "atheist," you mean "someone who has no God." But what God does this refer to? Often we are only talking about an image, which has been taught to us. One can be an atheist in this sense, and still believe in Life, which inhabits us. But God is Life. Christ himself said: "I am the Truth and the Life." Often, words become fixations: "I am an atheist, I am this, I am that . . ." What is important is to observe what qualities of existence we are prepared to welcome, whether we can discover the openness in Being. That, which eludes us or transcends us, is nonetheless precious.

There are atheists whose rejection of God is really a rejection of any image or name for the ultimate Reality. Yet this does not prevent them from living in intimacy with transcendent Reality, which is beyond the limits of their ego. There are paths that eschew all religion and tradition. Yet the role of a tradition or religion is to lead us to this same experience of Reality.

**Then these people are agnostics?**
Why must we always label our ways of being? All human beings, however they are labeled, have access to the Reality of which we are speaking. Every human being has a heart, and this heart can expand through love. Every human being has an intelligence, which can see clearly. Every human being can open his or her humanity to that which transcends humanity. To do this is to become truly human.

This is what Nietzsche really meant when he said "Man is a bridge . . ." A bridge is made to be crossed over. We become Human to the extent that we open to what is more than human. To be closed to this is not to be fully human. We become fully human in our capacity to open to transcendence. To be open is not to be closed within our mortal nature. But this opening is a free choice. One is free to choose to imprison oneself in one's ego, in one's being that is made to die.

Sometimes this ego becomes fed up with its own human suffering, unhappiness, and worries. Then comes a decision to open to reality in a different way. What we are suggesting here is to try this different way, to see that it can make you happier. Find out for yourself!

# SEVENTEEN

# FOUR NEGATIVE ACTIONS
# OF SPEECH

L et us look at our words and the states of mind that are behind them. There are four ways of misusing speech.

## LYING

Why do we lie? To protect our image, to advance ourselves: always the same ego-mechanism. Let us begin by trying to rid our lives of "what is not," so as to be able to speak "what is."

Once I asked the Dalai-Lama: "What is *nirvana*?"

"What is, is. What is not, is not," he replied.

These words were also spoken by the Buddha. I confess I was a little disappointed by this quotation—I had been hoping for something more metaphysical. To me, the word *nirvana* evoked something marvelous. Yet he was saying that is was simply seeing things as they are.

In the Gospels, Jesus says: "Let your yes be yes, let your no be no." We have spoken of the elegant Latin version: *Est est, non est non est*. All else is superfluous, mental games, illusion. To speak of things as they are, neither more nor less. Often when we speak, especially when we are talking about ourselves, we add or subtract things.

Humility does not consist in removing things but in neither adding nor subtracting.


## ILL WILL

The second form of negative speech is using words that create disharmony, stir up conflict, and spread ill will.

Language is a wondrous gift, the very organ of relationship, and communication with each other. Without it, the Buddha would not have been able to share his experience, nor the Christ able to communicate the creative Logos that inhabited him. Using words, we can heal, and even save lives—there are words, which save us, encouraging us to stand upright, and get back on the path; and there are other words, which kill us. Language is a dangerous gift! The briefest of phrases, spoken to us when we are very young, can become terrible burdens, which we drag around for the rest of our lives: "You'll never amount to anything!" Or "No matter what you do, it goes wrong!"

It is extremely important to be careful about what we say. This vigilance energizes our concrete, everyday practice. Jesus places great emphasis on this when he says that every false word we speak shall be counted on the Day of Judgment. This also includes spreading rumors. "They say that . . ." Very few of our words are grounded in the real . . .

When we listen to words, we should also ask what their real basis is. Have spreaders of ill will managed to tarnish our image of someone with a few words that damage their reputation? Rumors can even kill. There are well-documented cases of suicide that were the direct result of false allegations and slander.

"Words come out of the mouth from an overflowing of the heart." This indicates that we can know someone from the way they speak. When people speak of others, they reveal more of themselves than of others, describing their own state of mind through their vision of the other. This is good psychology, and it is also rather obvious! This is also why Jesus said, "Judge not, lest you be judged." Your own judgment indicates how you should be judged.

The emphasis on this, which we find in the Gospels, can also be found in the words of the Buddha: "Be vigilant about your language." Words can enlighten, but they can also destroy. St. James said: "He who masters his speech, masters his body." Our tongue is as difficult to master as a dragon's, for it can start fires. Paying attention to all negative speech (or lies, slander, and gossip, disguised as information) is an exercise of mastery of our whole being, including our body.

Compassion is lucid, never indulgent. When something needs to be said, say it. But avoid the extremes of mincing words, or using words that spread dissension and disharmony. It is not necessary to pour oil on the fire, to counter ill will with more ill will. Nor can we count on silence as an easy way out of every difficult situation. Just as words can kill, so can certain silences.

Hence we must find not only the right words but also the right silence.

On the way of compassion, we discover the extent to which words can be useless, if not harmful. We must learn to avoid both and be very clear about whom we are really speaking to, as well as what we are really saying.

## INSULT

The third type of negative speech consists of words used as a form of aggression, which can wound. The bodhisattva never resorts to insult. The same is true of the Servant in the Bible. In Isaiah, it is said: "He never raises his voice in the street . . . he never crushes a wick that is still burning."

This nonviolence of speech does not imply lack of firmness. Words do not have to be violent in order to carry authority and energy, and to be firm, clear, and concise. What good is there in adding the contempt and violence that are carried by insult? It only seeks to humiliate, slander, or crush the other. It can only impede communication. Insult is the end of all listening, the end of a possible relationship. In the path of awakening, one speaks one's mind firmly and truly, but one avoids any tone or form of insult. One eschews any violence of speech that could kill dialogue or destroy another.

## CHATTER

The fourth kind of negative speech is gossip, or chatter. For the bodhisattva, this is a waste of energy. In Jungian terms, indulgence in chatter is characteristic of a poorly-integrated *anima*. Whether we are male or female, when the feminine dimension in us is poorly integrated, it results in acts of speech, which are sterile, uncreative, futile, repetitious—as Shakespeare put it: "much ado about nothing."

Such futility of speech is often a sign of anxiety, because one cannot bear silence—in some groups of people, what a strange apprehension and disquiet appears, when there is too much silence! For such people, it is difficult to see that silence is not necessarily negative; it is difficult to accept the possibility of simply enjoying each other's company, with nothing to say. The fear of emptiness compels some people to fill this silence. Chatter fills emptiness with meaninglessness.

On the other hand, there is no systematic rule that can tell us when to speak and when to be silent. For example, it can be good to break certain silences, even with banalities, when they are charged with unspoken negativity or fear. A smile or a reassuring word then changes the atmosphere, making true silence possible. This can happen in a waiting room, for instance, when an unfriendly, or even hostile, silence somehow appears. A few simple, friendly words can change everything—and the silence that follows is of a totally different order. This is because goodwill has been established.

Yet much energy can be wasted in chatter. This not only prevents us from speaking true words but from hearing them.

These four types of negative speech (lying, ill-will, insult, and chatter) are the causes of much pain and destruction. Among the Desert Fathers, there was a proverb: "Go ahead, talk, talk! You'll still have something left to say."

There is a story from this same tradition, about a young novice with a sharp tongue, who could not resist making "comments" about the other monks. One day his Elder told him to go fetch a guinea hen. When he returned with it, the Elder told him to pluck it. The novice obeyed, and when he was finished, the Elder said:

"Now, put all the feathers back on it."

Bewildered, the novice finally protested: "But it's already plucked! I can't put the feathers back!"

"Correct," the Elder replied, "and it's the same when you say bad things about your brothers. You pluck away at their reputation, and if you keep on, it may be lost forever."

Thus when we criticize others, we "pluck" them. We must realize that there is always a risk that we are doing something that may be irreparable. Technically, this is not murder, but little stabs of the knife can kill slowly.

# EIGHTEEN

# FOUR POSITIVE ACTIONS OF SPEECH

## SPEAKING HONESTLY

This begins with speaking frankly, saying what one thinks, yet remembering that we are limited by our way of seeing and interpreting things. A contemporary scientist might say: "What I call *truth* is an interpretation of reality through more or less subtle instruments. But reality is infinitely greater than I can grasp."

But often, we are really saying: "What I think is the truth and nothing but the truth." Yet an honest and frank attitude is one that remains keenly aware of the limits of our knowledge, and of what we interpret as reality.

## SPEAKING FOR THE GOOD

The second way is speaking words, which bring about harmony. It consists of speaking of what is good about people, instead of what is wrong with them. For some people this is an almost impossible exercise, for they have become totally habituated to speaking critically. We all seem to have a special talent for finding critical things to say about the world, about others, and about ourselves!

Of course this must not be forced, for then such speech becomes hollow. We must develop an interest in seeing the best qualities of another person. From this positive standpoint, we can better understand all their actions. This was the practice of St. Dominic, founder of the Dominican order. "Never criticize an absent brother." One may speak frankly to him about a disagreement but only in his presence, when he is able to defend himself. This is an attitude of fairness.

## MAINTAINING A SPACE OF LISTENING

This third type of positive speech not only avoids aggressive or hurtful words, it also avoids overwhelming others with long-winded verbiage. It always keeps a space of listening. We have all met people who do not listen—they talk endlessly, and we feel submerged in a flood of words, and drowned by them.

In this attitude, whenever you are speaking, you are also listening. You are speaking to another being. Then there will be a space for their response.

## SPEAKING CLEARLY AND CONCISELY

The fourth type of good speech requires ridding ourselves of superfluous words, which in turn requires the courage of silence. Then we can speak clearly and to the point. This exercise also presupposes a certain quality of the heart. With this quality, our motivation in speaking is not to shine, to be admired, to display our intelligence. We speak because we desire to be understood, to understand others, and to bring out the intelligence in them. It is true that there are forms of knowledge, which demand a special vocabulary, which not everyone understands. But it is also true that the ego loves an excuse to demonstrate that it knows something others do not know.

Physicians, scientists, or philosophers often resort to sophisticated language, which seems to put them "in the know." But even in this case, clear and concise speaking implies sympathy and an awareness of nuances in language, so as to be understood by others. One can feel from the way such a person speaks, where their heart is—whether or not their true desire is to communicate and to share their learning. With sympathy of the heart, one finds ways to render difficult and complex subjects comprehensible by nonspecialists. Without it, people use their knowledge to impress or dominate others, making them feel inferior because of their ignorance, and preventing them from overcoming it.

No way of compassion can consist merely of vowing to save all beings. It must involve concrete actions, especially in our acts of speech. Vigilance in speech also contributes to the welfare of all beings. Even if we cannot yet celebrate life through our words, we can at least express reverence for it, refraining from speaking in ways that pollute it.

**Question: Why is it that our minds seem to tend toward critical and damaging words instead of positive and beneficial ones?**
Let us first notice how we use the word "critical." Originally, it referred to a mind capable of discrimination, not one with a tendency toward continual disparagement. We must distinguish between *critique,* in this sense, and criticism, which seeks to disparage and destroy.

Why do we find pleasure in destroying? Where does this state of mind come from? There is no general answer, only particular cases. Perhaps it is because we have been conditioned to have a fundamental attitude of mistrust, and we constantly indulge in criticism because of the weight of repetitive memories, which seem to justify this. In other words, a fundamental attitude of goodwill and trust has been eclipsed. By criticizing something we place ourselves above it. Again, this is based on an ego, which needs constant reassurance, and exalts itself at the expense of others.

The compassionate person does not require other people to be stupid, in order to be intelligent. Their intelligence is for everyone, so as to have a world in which there is less ignorance. If we cannot make ourselves understood by others, it is because our truth has not been skillfully communicated. Our knowledge and lucidity have not been transmitted.

The ego, which affirms itself at the expense of others, renders them more stupid and encloses them in their ignorance; and ignorance is suffering. When we encounter someone who has no sense of the meaning of life, or why they are here, we encounter someone who is suffering. Our intelligence can add to their suffering; or it can, on the contrary, help them to get out of it.

The way of compassion invites us to go beyond our ego, that bundle of memories of which "we" are made. When we go beyond it, then there is no one left to accuse or be accused. Then we become able to assume responsibility (as Dostoyevsky and Lévinas might say) "for everything and for everyone."

How can we get beyond this incessantly criticizing state of mind? A key is suggested in some expressions of popular wisdom, such as "Turn your tongue around in your mouth seven times before you speak." This physical exercise can actually make our tongue more conscious and make us more conscious of the sounds and words that come out of our mouth. Little by little, we can learn to let go of negative and hurtful words, which ultimately destroy others and ourselves.

---

## A MOMENT OF MEDITATION

*Let us offer ourselves five minutes of beautiful silence. Not because we "don't know what to say," but because we have the right to be silent.*

*There is nothing wrong with speech, but it can be useless or harmful.*

*Lead us toward a speech, which is as beautiful as silence, and toward a silence, which is as beautiful as the sweetest and truest of words.*

*The source of all speech is the Breath.*

*Let us approach this source of words, which is in the Breath, and this source of the Breath, which is the beginning of inspiration. At the end comes expiration, breathing out, the silence of Presence.*

# NINETEEN

---

# THREE NEGATIVE ACTIONS OF THE MIND

O n this way of compassion, it will be helpful to further observe the three negative and positive actions of the mind.

## POSSESSIVENESS

This first action of the mind comes from attachment. For example, suppose I have a watch to which I am attached. Consider what happens on a physical level when I grasp it tightly: I still have the watch, but I no longer have a free hand, because it is distorted and very occupied. It is useful to observe this physical tightening and rigidity of our hands. This can sometimes be seen in dying people who grasp their bedsheets, stiffening their whole bodies, all the way to their feet.

Health is the power to open or to close. Yet sometimes we swing from one extreme to another. If I decide it is "bad" to grasp, then instead of true detachment, I go to the extreme of indifference. The limp, open hand is incapable of grasping, just as the grasping hand with the watch cannot open. A healthy hand is able to grasp something in order to open again so as to give it. It can open and close easily, in giving and receiving.

The same is true of the mind. We must learn to have a more flexible grasp and embrace: firm when necessary but ready to lighten and let go as well. We must also not enclose ourselves in exclusive relationships, rejecting others, as happens in certain families. The mind as well as the heart must be open, lightening its grasp. But this does not mean going to extremes of claiming to "love everyone." When people make such claims, one often suspects that in reality they are unable to love anyone.

We must be able to receive, to embrace, and to take, as well as to give. The heart can close in an embrace around a particular beloved, yet without any possession or oppression. We must be able to open without losing ourselves, and set limits without imprisoning ourselves.

## ANTAGONISM

The second negative aspect of mind is antagonism. We have all met people who seem to operate from an a priori of antagonism: "Obviously, that's wrong! Obviously, it won't work! Obviously, you are an idiot! Obviously . . ." Whatever the circumstances, this is a poison of the mind.

## FIXATING ON CONCEPTS

To fixate on concepts is to have an inflexible mind, which is another form of poison. What is true at one time may not be true at another time. Reality changes, yet one remains fixed. The mind and heart thus grasp tightly to ideas, in a similar way to the hand. "Tight-fistedness" clearly relates to the mind and heart more than to the hand. This also applies to one's ideas. Being unwilling to change them is a harmful state of mind, which breeds unhappiness. As the saying goes, ideas are like clothes: change them often if you wish to keep them clean.

It is helpful to observe our inflexibility of body, emotions, and thoughts. Exactly where are our "tight" places? Perhaps the American expression "redneck" also suggests an excess of blood that stiffens the neck, making the head less flexible! In any case, it is an attitude, which holds rigidly onto a certain concept of reality, imprisoning oneself and others within it. One ceases to listen to other ideas, and in closing around one's concept, one becomes closed-minded.

The Bible uses the metaphor of "stiff-necked." In general, the Bible avoids abstractions, and often resorts to body-based metaphors. Hence a stiff neck implies a reduced field of vision. One sees only what is directly in front, as if wearing blinders.

On the way of compassion, possessiveness, antagonism, and closed-mindedness are seen as poisons of the mind, and poisons in the world.

# TWENTY

# THREE POSITIVE ACTIONS
# OF THE MIND

## SATISFACTION

Now we consider the positive antidotes for the negative qualities. Satisfaction is the antidote for possessiveness. This means being content with what you have. As the proverb goes, "Want what you get, and you will get what you want." To love and desire what one has—this corresponds to *samtosha* in Sanskrit, sometimes translated as "contentment." There are people who are never content with what they have, who always look for happiness elsewhere, or in the future. Others are happy with only a drink of water, a ray of sunshine, a smile . . .

In contrast to possessiveness, which is never content with what it has, there is a kind of satisfaction (not to be confused with self-satisfaction), which is based on gratitude for what one has been given. This sense of gratitude is something that can and must be developed in us. Only when we acknowledge what has been given to us, can we truly give.

## GOODWILL

This is clearly the attitude we need to develop as an antidote for antagonism: to wish others well, to be attentive to them, to operate from an a priori of goodwill. When everyone tells me how dishonest a certain person is, it is true that I am forewarned so as not to be "taken" by him or her; but at the same time I must also cultivate my a priori of goodwill toward that person. This could even help them not to be dishonest.

How can people ever trust themselves, when others heap only mistrust upon them? Sensing your negative attitude toward them, they respond exactly in kind. When you see someone as fundamentally dishonest, you actually encourage them to maintain their role of dishonesty. But when you look clearly and unsentimentally into that part of their being, which is always truthful, knowing that it is there, you empower them to act honestly. You might even wind up giving the keys to your house to a thief, in complete confidence! But of course there can be no generalizations here. We must experience and verify this for ourselves.

These examples are somewhat oversimplified. *Policies* of goodwill do not always work. You may offer complete trust to your child, and he or she may betray it. But at least you will have given it. The role of parents is not an easy one because they know things that their children do not. This gives rise to a tendency to do things for them, thereby depriving them of the experience of learning by making their own mistakes.

Goodwill means vigilant awareness of your trust in others. We can still offer goodwill to others, no matter how badly they behave, by seeing the possibility of good deep within them. On some level they will sense this benevolent regard, they will feel recognized and more worthy. There are some people whose regard makes us into an object, reducing us and shriveling us. Other regards, on the contrary, make us feel wonderful because the person sees the essential goodness in us.

When you turn this positive regard upon someone, you give rise to goodness in that person. To have been regarded like this even once by a saint or a bodhisattva, can bring about a rebirth of confidence in ourselves.

While others were already stoning the adulterous woman with their hard regards, the Christ simply saw a suffering being who had lost touch with the love within her and looked in vain for it elsewhere. Likewise, when the other disciples saw Matthew as a Roman collaborator, because he collected taxes from his Jewish brothers to give to the occupiers, Jesus saw a man who had the potential to become a disciple.

This is the quality, which we must develop in ourselves. If we do not see others as fundamentally "owing" us anything, how can we be afraid that our trust in them is a fundamental mistake? It is always possible that they may betray our trust, since they are endowed with free will. But at least we know that we have not withheld from them this gift of trust, this chance, and done so in full consciousness.

## FLEXIBILITY OF MIND

This third quality is the antidote for closed-mindedness. It renounces the tendency to fight over words, knowing that words may have different meanings for different people. For some people, God is a powerful and intimate experience; for others it is a mere word, and one, which has poisoned their lives, being associated with people who oppressed them in the name of God. To be flexible is not to be bound by words, and to find ways to communicate to these people the experience, which is hidden by the word "God" or "Buddha."

Many people speak of love, but they do not mean the same thing by it. The reality of love demands that we be more precise. When another tells us that they love us, we sometimes realize that they do not love us in the way that we thought. This can lead to surprise: we may either be disappointed . . . or perhaps delighted!

A flexible mind uses language in order to communicate. It does not confine people with labels or other descriptions. The simple practice of adding formulas of politeness, such as "according to my understanding," "the way I see it," and so on, can actually help us to be more aware of our limits of perception. This will make us less rigid, less closed, less fanatical . . . Much blood has been shed over words, and a great deal of it over the word "God."

The flexible mind also seeks to understand the other and what they are trying to say. It also does not automatically assume that its way of seeing things is the best. It is a type of mind, which is able to say: "I am telling you what I think, what I have experienced, what I know—but I am not saying I am right. I have something to learn from you and from your disagreements with my opinions. You do not love in exactly the same way I do, and this is a good thing—otherwise, how could I learn from you? Your different way might offer me a dimension of which I am not aware."

Open-mindedness applies to both thinking and feeling. Few people have a truly open mind. What often goes under the name of open-mindedness is really a kind of mindlessness, a gullibility ready to believe all kinds of nonsense. Being flexible is not the same thing as lacking convictions!

Being flexible in one's convictions is being aware of what one really knows, and what one doesn't know. My love for the Buddha does not make me any less a Christian: my conviction of the beauty and grandeur of Christianity does not mean I have to denigrate the Buddha. I try to practice the teaching of the Gospels as I understand them, but that does not prevent me from finding Buddhism interesting. On the contrary, Buddhists have taught me something about how to practice the teaching of the Gospels. Love of one's enemies is at the heart of both traditions. They both teach us to try to love our enemies, to love what makes us afraid, and to love what makes us suffer.

I must repeat something, which will not be to everyone's liking: one of the most authentic Christians I have ever met, a man who truly practices the teaching of the Gospel, is the Dalai Lama. If anyone practices true love of one's enemies, it is the Dalai Lama. I have never heard a single harsh word of judgment from him about the Chinese. He combines this love with a refusal of any complacency regarding their unjust acts and works for the liberation of his people. He is someone who lives his tradition and his convictions fully, yet he is never closed toward others, even his enemies. He is even able to point out what is positive in them.

One day, he told me: "If it weren't for the Chinese, I wouldn't be talking to you right now. It's a good thing they kicked me out—otherwise you in the West might know less about Buddhism." Of course that does not mean it is right for the Tibetans to undergo such terrible sufferings and injustices—the Dalai Lama says this is unacceptable. But he says it with no hatred.

How do we practice compassion in the world of politics? It is the world of dominant power, and often a world of no respect for others. It is very rare to find a head of state who respects his enemy, naming the enemy as a usurper, yet doing so with no contempt, no hatred, and no violence . . . and it is just as rare among Christian politicians!

But not all Buddhists are such good Christians as the Dalai Lama! How does the teaching of compassion—whatever tradition it comes from—really help us to advance in our practice of it? I would hope that those who love the Gospels could also learn to practice goodwill, open-mindedness, and nonpossessiveness.

When one is firm in one's faith, genuinely grounded in one's tradition and one's culture, one has a basis for opening to others and recognizing the beautiful things about their faith. Having roots and being open are complementary, and reinforce each other.

**Question: How can we have goodwill when confronted with vulgarity and ugliness?**

We must learn to see ugliness with eyes of beauty. Dirty fingernails do not seem so disgusting when you see them with eyes of beauty. That does not mean you have to like them. The Christ said: "Love your enemies." He did not say: "Fall in love with your enemies." We must not mix and confuse things. You are not being asked to love what you consider ugly but simply to not add your negative judgments to the situation, which only reinforces the feeling of ugliness. If you fixate on a woman's dirty fingernails, you may miss her beautiful eyes or body. We see things according to our attitude. Does a love of beauty really inform the way you see? It is my belief that if we truly see things through the eyes of a heart that loves beauty, we will be able to find it in everything, even a tiny seed.

# TWENTY-ONE

# PATIENCE

Patience is essential to the way of compassion. This goes far beyond simply enduring, tolerating, or "stomaching" heavy moments. It is also a certain transparence, a certain permeability that is linked to intelligence. The more we develop this quality of intelligence, the more patient we will naturally become. Also, our awareness of the impermanence of all things reminds us that this, too, will pass.

It was Plato who said: "To understand everything is to forgive everything." In this aphorism, I detect a beautiful invitation to patience, as well as forgiveness. To understand others is to understand the way, which has brought them to this situation. Then we become more patient and kind toward them.

But before we dare to speak of patience, we should first observe our own impatience. How do we react when the bus is late, or when they are late in serving us at the restaurant? This kind of observation can bring us back to reality! But instead of telling ourselves to calm down, we would do better to remind ourselves to return to the roots of our being. That is where real calm is to be found. Others are still there, they are still disappointing us, suffering is still there—yet the only way it can pass more quickly is by saying *Yes* to *what is.* Saying *No* will only make the suffering last longer.

In Hebrew, the root of the word "to be patient" means "to have large nostrils." This means breathing deeply. To be patient is to have a breath, which is great and deep. Just observe how you breathe when you are impatient. When this turns into anger, your breathing becomes much shorter. You lose breath: you become out of breath, and "out of your mind." The development of patience is greatly aided by developing the out-breath. When you find yourself at odds with the world, when your shoulders start to hunch down, and you feel like you could explode: breathe out . . . and breathe out again!

There is nothing abstract about patience. It is deeply related to our body, our breathing, right down to our feet. To be patient is often to get back on a sound footing, to find one's ground, to feel it beneath one's feet, so as not to be carried away by emotion. When we are able to breathe deeply, and breathe out a long breath, we are able to listen to others, to be more patient.

TWENTY-TWO

# ENERGY

The way of compassion is also a way of healing. One must have strength in order to be openhearted, kind, and benevolent. Kindness is a virtue for the strong. Otherwise, it degenerates into softness.

Jesus speaks of kindness and humility of the heart. But Jesus is strong, a man with energy—how else could he overturn the tables of the money changers? Kindness is the expression of a strength, which no longer needs to prove itself. If we have lingering doubts about our strength (or intelligence), we want to display it to others, so as to prove ourselves. But when we are attentive to reality, to what is happening, and feel this energy within us, we have no need to show it.

The way of compassion requires a great deal of energy, but if we try to live it with the energy of the separate self, we will soon become exhausted. How can this energy be developed? A skillful means of recharging ourselves and getting back into tune with a higher energy is the practice of retreat and meditation. When we find a certain person unbearable—impossible to put up with any longer—we must accept that it is indeed impossible for the ego, and ask for help from something greater and stronger within us. It may be our lot to bear "inhuman" burdens, yet there is something beyond the human within us, something, which can bear these burdens, yet surpasses our understanding.

The Energy, which we must develop within us, is an Energy that is infinite. This is seen in action in the lives of people who somehow get through desperate situations, amazed that they were capable of such a thing. What made it possible was their contact with a source of energy, which transcends them, a vitality, which overflows the limits of what is ordinarily possible.

Courage, as well as strength, is needed on this path. Without energy one can do nothing, and without courage, we cannot begin anew each day, letting go of any notion of acquisition. This applies both to worldly and to spiritual endeavors.

# TWENTY-THREE

# MEDITATION

Meditation is the practice of sitting silently. In it, we rediscover the perfections previously developed: time, body, discipline, mind. We observe ourselves and develop positive qualities. Again, this requires great patience and energy.

### A MOMENT OF MEDITATION

*Sit in the posture that is best for you.*

*If you are not used to meditating regularly, let me recall the importance of a well-anchored position. The spine should be as straight as possible, and the shoulders relaxed.*

*If too many thoughts come and go, just come back to awareness of your breathing or perhaps to an invocation, which is helpful and familiar to you.*

*Experience this time of meditation with no goal in mind, no seeking of benefits, no self-interest at all. Forget any desire for experiences of ecstasy, inner fire, and so on. Forget also any desire for consolation or reassurance. Yet do not refuse such experiences if they come. They may or may not come, and they will surely pass.*

*Experience this time of meditation not just for yourself but also for the good of all beings.*

*Let us find inspiration in this passage from Shantideva, so as to welcome what is, to welcome whatever happens, while wishing peace and happiness for all beings:*

*Just as earth and other elements are useful in various ways to innumerable sentient beings dwelling throughout infinite space, so may I be in various ways a source of life for the sentient beings present throughout space until they are liberated.*

*Just as a blind man finds a jewel amongst heaps of rubbish, so this spirit of Awakening has somehow arisen in me.*

*It is the elixir of life produced to vanquish death in the world. It is an inexhaustible treasure eliminating the poverty of the world.*

*It is the supreme medicine that alleviates the illness of the world. It is the tree of rest for beings exhausted from wandering on the pathways of mundane existence.*

*It is the universal bridge for all travelers on their crossing over miserable states of existence. It is the rising moon of the mind that soothes the mental afflictions of the world.*

*It is the great sun dispelling the darkness of the world's ignorance. It is the fresh butter formed from churning the milk of Dharma.*

*For the caravan of beings traveling on the path to mundane existence and starving for the meal of happiness, it is the feast of happiness that satisfies all sentient beings who have come as guests.*

*Today, in the presence of all saints, I invite the world to the state of awakening and peace. For this, I am ready to take on the burden of all sufferings. I am resolved in this, I will endure it. I will not disavow it, nor flee it. I do not tremble from fear. I am not afraid, nor do I turn back, nor become discouraged. How can this be? Because this is my vow.*

———————————

This practice goes against the grain of the ego in two of its primary modes of operation: possessiveness and fear. It also goes against today's widespread preaching of meditation as a tool for personal advancement, health, and well-being. The ego is capable of possessiveness, not only toward persons and things but toward spiritual states as well. In this practice, whatever happens to us does not belong to us. It leads to a sort of unfreezing, a fluidity of the ego and the separate self. If something good happens to us, let it happen, let it pass, let us offer it up for the good of all living beings.

The second aspect is perhaps the most difficult: to take upon one-self all suffering, with resolve to endure it all . . . this is only natural, for we are afraid of suffering. But this practice aims to deliver us from one of the most fundamental of all our fears. In this form of meditation, we strive to overcome our fear of impurity and of death. When suffering arises during this meditation, the practice is to let it pass without fear or aversion, which will only reinforce it. Also, we accept this suffering not as ours, nor for us, but as a participation in the suffering of all beings.

This meditation practice also prepares us for a way of life, which is very different from the usual habits of ego-based life, which involve constant grasping, possessiveness, self-protection, habits of avoidance, and defensiveness toward anything painful or disagreeable. But what good is a life lived in defense against suffering? It will happen anyway! Ego-based life, with its permanent fear of suffering, can develop into anxiety and anguish, to the point of madness. The more we combat suf-fering, the more we are imprisoned by it, and the more paranoid we are likely to become. We can even develop the impression that everything is against us, pursuing us in order to destroy us.

To say *Yes* to suffering, to the fact of its existence, can at least cure us of this pathology. If we are capable of this *Yes*—beginning with the annoyances of everyday life—we will find that this suffering curiously diminishes, and the fear along with it. We must become capable of accepting the disagreeable along with the agreeable. This is a very high form of practice, requiring a great maturity of heart and mind. It would be wrong to consider it as a simple thing.

In certain weekend workshops, we can learn techniques to bring out repressed emotions, using screams and movements, which break down our character armor, so as to dislodge the packets of condensed memories that have been causing so much suffering in us. And then what happens Monday morning? Often we find that with our armor gone, we can barely stand up. This is deeply significant, for it shows to what extent we rely on our defenses and our armor in order to stand firm. Our ego causes us to live constantly on the defensive, and without these defenses, we are weak and disoriented in the world.

I have nothing against skillful means of removing our armor, but only if it is replaced with an inner backbone! This is what is missing in many therapeutic practices: they know how to work on defenses, but they do nothing to build strength of character—backbone—to replace the loss of defenses.

We must never forget that the core of the approach we are speaking of here is the fact that we carry within us the essence of awakening, the presence of Life. If we happen to be Buddhist, we will call this the presence of the Buddha-nature, a capacity to transform things through knowledge and compassion. If we are Christian, awakening to the presence of the inner Christ will empower us to let go of our defenses and the whole structure of the ego. Otherwise, it would be folly to take on the sufferings of the world! They would overwhelm us immediately, in a grave sickness not unlike those terrible states where we identify with the symptoms that torture us.

The practice we need is one in which we can live in an attitude of nondefensiveness, nonduality, and nonparanoia, because we are solidly grounded in the presence of the Self. Then we know directly that we have within us this possibility of compassionate energy, which makes us fearless in the face of suffering. It is the alchemical fire, which can transmute the lead of hardships. Then we can actually welcome the most disagreeable, toxic, harmful, impure, and unspeakable experiences. They will only further stoke the fire that radiates light.

This meditation is a fearlessness in the face of death, suffering, and calamity. It is only possible because we accept and recognize in ourselves this power of transformation. Meditation practice recenters us in this energy, compassion, and clarity, which is not our separate self but Life within us.

This life and light may take the form of the Buddha and his fearless, living light and truth; or it may take the form of Jesus of Nazareth, who incarnates in all his actions this fearlessness in the face of suffering, who is able to take upon himself the sufferings and negativities of the world and transform them.

> May I be an inexhaustible treasure for the poor, may I be ready to serve them in any way they ask.
>
> In all my future incarnations, I hereby abandon all rewards and merits, which may be due to me, so that all beings may realize their true goal. Nirvana is abandoning everything, and my soul aspires to this deliverance. Since I abandon everything, I do best to offer it to others.
>
> I offer my body to the enjoyment of all beings, though they beat it, violate it, and cover it with dust, though they make a toy of my body, an object of amusement and derision. I have given them my body, and it matters not to me what they do with it, as long as it is not harmful to any being.
>
> If another being's heart is angry and hostile toward me, may even that help to realize the happiness of all beings. May those who abuse and insult me rally me to work for the awakening of all beings.
>
> May I be a protector of the abandoned ones, a guide for those who are on the path, may I be a bridge and a boat for those who desire to reach the other shore. May I be a lamp for those who have none, a bed for those who have no place to sleep, the servant of those who need a servant. May I be a miracle-stone, a healing plant, the tree of wishes, and the cow of desires.

In these astonishing Eastern texts, we find echoes of Christian mystical writings. But we must read them with discrimination, so as to avoid any sort of masochistic interpretation. They are not saying we should seek suffering but that we should prepare ourselves for it, conquering it to the point of fearlessly offering one's body, one's actions, one's speech, and one's teaching, for the benefit of others. Openness to others and being for others goes far beyond the separate self, and one tastes a quality of being, and a presence of Being in us, which can never be taken from us, which is indestructible.

Thus I can give my body, insofar as I know this indestructible Being, which is in me, but which is independent of the body. "Neither fear those who destroy this body, for there is something in you that cannot be destroyed, a light, which darkness cannot touch," as the Gospel says.

> Thus I fear not darkness, because I know. But first I must have experienced the certainty of this Presence in me, which neither death nor suffering can destroy. When we have touched this, we are able to enter the way of compassion.

The above vow gives a direction and an orientation to the heart. Knowing that we are not here merely to seek our own well-being and the well-being of those close to us, knowing that we cannot be satisfied while others are unhappy, opens the heart. To have this knowledge is to awaken to a certain quality incarnated by the Buddha and the Christ. The bodhisattvas and saints are human beings who have lived in space-time and in history like us, who have been plunged into the same human current as we have. Surely, it is possible for us as well.

**Question: Is it always appropriate to take on another's suffering? Sometimes it would seem best to return it, so they can face up to it. Many therapists know this principle of receiving suffering but only so as to give it back to the patient, so that they can work on it. What would a bodhisattva say about this?**
There is some confusion here about the meaning of "taking on" suffering. The bodhisattva never takes on suffering so as to keep it—in fact, that would be pathological, because the personality would be overwhelmed by it. Perhaps "taking on" is a bad translation. To "take" suffering suggests holding on to it, to own it, and nothing could be further

from the bodhisattva path. This recalls the tendency to wrongly interpret this path as having an element of masochism. It is true that there
are pathological cases of sadism or masochism, which seek pleasure in
suffering. Compassion is not a pathology!

Perhaps we should seek a better terminology. If you find "taking
on" objectionable, then I suggest you find a better way of expressing it
for you. I would prefer to say something like "welcoming through oneself" in relation to another's suffering. We welcome it because the other
is there, and their suffering is a fact. But we must not stop there—we
must allow the suffering to pass through us.

While it is passing through us, it makes us feel pain, even in our
body. We are touched by this suffering, which is real. For example, we
may empathetically feel a fever, which is not ours, when confronted
with a sick person who "discharges" on us. But this energetic, physical
discomfort is not ours. We can accept a moment of being "contaminated" by another's suffering, but that does not prevent us from letting
it pass through very quickly. This fever, this suffering, this discomfort
will pass, precisely because it is not the small "me" that welcomes it, and
I do not appropriate it as part of my personality.

A certain inner distance is necessary. This perspective of distance
allows us to clearly distinguish ourselves from the other person and
their suffering, avoiding any confusion. Otherwise, we can harm ourselves, especially if we are dealing with severe cases. Whether psychic or
physical, every illness has a certain "contagious" quality. We need not
fear this quality. In fact, to fear it is to make it more dangerous.

You ask if we should "return" the suffering to the other. No, not if
our attitude is one of "Sorry, it's your problem, not mine. I can't solve it,
you have to deal with it." On the other hand, it may be good to remind
a person of their responsibility. We all know cases where people have
an unhealthy habit of asking for help, so as to avoid dealing with their
problems. But a true attitude of compassion does not "return" suffering
to a person overwhelmed by it. Instead, it returns it to the Earth, to the
Universe, to the sources of life. In this attitude, we welcome suffering,

allowing it to pass through us, confiding it to God (or whatever word one prefers for the ultimate Reality), returning it to the chasms of light of an infinite Love. Capable of operating through us (or beyond us), it is this Being who receives suffering and brings about the necessary transformations of it.

To welcome suffering is not to keep it but to let it pass. It is true that this requires that we develop a certain skill, so as not to become a kind of human garbage can. This is of course not possible for anyone who experiences pleasure and curiosity in hearing another's painful, cruel, and ugly memories exposed. We must keep that fire alive in us, a fire that can transform the worst psychic sewage. In the end, it is joy that will overcome. "Carry each others' burdens," St. Paul said. But again, to carry is not to keep, nor to nurture.

In several traditions, we encounter the image of the sponge, as a metaphor for the compassionate person. A sponge can become full with another's suffering—and it must never forget to empty itself! To fail to empty oneself is to risk living in confusion, especially when it turns out that another's suffering has resemblances to our own. This is the time for meditation, and for offering up the suffering.

As long as we center ourselves in transcendence, in that endless depth of light and peace within us, our sponge is immersed in the ocean of life and love. When it has emptied itself of suffering, it fills itself with the water of life and clarity. From this space of beatitude and inner happiness we can then offer our sponge to heal wounds, to give a little peace and light to others. This can happen with only a gesture or a word. It can also happen by simply being present in silence and in peace. Then comes a time for emptying our sponge once more, so as to receive all sorts of negativity and anguish . . . . and then to empty it again and again. This metaphor recalls the rhythm of breathing in (welcoming), and breathing out (giving).

If you visit a severely ill or dying person, take a moment of meditation to "recharge" yourself before entering their room. Something in you will radiate naturally, as if you were gently squeezing your "sponge."

You will be a light, which can at least radiate in the darkness, if not dispel it.

The sponge represents your heart: your body-mind purified of self-indulgence, and fearless in the face of others' suffering. Often our heart is more like a stone than a sponge. But this heart of stone can melt and become receptive to pain along with pleasure, to fear along with love, to anguish along with joy. Espousing the Real, it is capable of welcoming the worst as well as the best.

This practice leads us into the way of compassion. Each of us, in our own way, welcomes the world's suffering, and gives back a little of that peace, which is not "ours," but which we can give. Since it does not belong to us, no one can ever take it away from us.

The way of compassion is a real transformation, and must not be reduced to a mere vow or a utopian dream. It demands paying attention to every kind of behavior, from bulimia to a tendency to worry, and this awareness must penetrate right down to our basic anguish, related to our obsession with objects of consciousness (whether gross or subtle), and our lack of presence of the subject of consciousness, which is who we are. We must refrain from judging such behaviors as "wrong" but simply witness them as a form of suffering, a sense of insecurity from which we yearn to be free. Then something begins to let go, to stop grasping, and to stop identifying oneself with one's habits of behavior. The ability to give is liberated in us, and the heart comes alive. We no longer look to external authority to tell us to do something or not do it, because our doing springs from the depths of the heart.

A moment comes in our life when all that we have accumulated becomes too heavy, and we realize that our desire to possess another prevents us from giving to them. The more we try to get others to love us, the more they want to flee. When we stop inwardly saying "Love me," we say "I love you, but you have the right not to love me." Then others feel their freedom to express themselves and are more likely to come to us.

Thus we free ourselves of the constant state of expectation and demand, realizing that we have a capacity to give, no matter how poor and deprived we are. It is the recognition of our inner wealth that allows the transformation to take place. St. Seraphim of Sarov said: "Find inner peace, and a multitude of beings will be saved along with you." This peace is not "mine" but the very peace of Being. The very fact that we are able to be ourselves within this peace can be felt by all that surrounds us.

---

### A MOMENT OF MEDITATION

*Let us take five minutes to simply be here. But notice that this "here" is an immensity without limits, reaching far beyond our own bodies, and any tendency to enclose it physically.*

*The space inside a jug is also the space that fills the universe. Let us approach the experience of it with no fear of opening to this space. We have nothing to protect, nothing to defend. What is, Is.*

*The Being within us cannot be grasped or taken from us. No one can possess this Light.*

*Let it be, let us breathe this Presence.*

---

To open and let go of your limits is not to lose them. There are some pathologies, which are characterized by a loss of any sense of limits, sometimes even including the body. If you have ever accompanied certain people who are suffering, you may have noticed that they have a problem of fear of loss of limits, loss of identity, and loss of form. They must first be reminded of their identity, their form, and their limits.

I see no need for conflict between different approaches in this matter. To open the space within the jug does not mean breaking it. Our aim is not to destroy the ego, for the ego is needed in order to go beyond it. The ego is the form with which we are identified, built from our bodily form and our memories. But this form is not the totality of who we are, and it is not necessary to shatter it in order to stop being enclosed within it.

The goal of the way of compassion is to lead us beyond ego, and this presupposes a certain maturity. It is not a teaching for children, for they are still in the process of constructing an ego, a way of differentiating themselves, beginning with mother, and later with the environment. There must be a successfully formed ego before it can be transcended. To try to skip this step is to fall into a pseudotranscendence of ego, which is a form of pathology.

Psychotherapy seeks to strengthen the form of someone who lacks it, to give a sense of grounding to someone who has lost her sense of identity. When this identity is recovered, then they can open and go beyond it. Hence there is no need to oppose psychology and spirituality. They can and should work together, and this can prevent errors in both domains.

To have a strong ego, well adapted to a sick world, is not yet to be healthy. Spirituality reminds us of a world beyond that of ego. But we can only transcend what we have accepted and acquired. We accept that we have an ego and a form. We are the children of our families, but we have the ability to go beyond this, to take a step further.

The way to the Self must pass through the self. There is no skipping steps here—otherwise, we risk dissolution, losing our limits but never transcending them. This would amount to a practice of discarnation—but the true path begins with incarnating well—accepting our form, before opening this incarnation to transfiguration and resurrection.

**Question: Is meditation meant to help us land, or to help us take off?**

I believe that true meditation is both. But one must make a good landing first, and that is a long path in itself. It is not difficult to leave the body, especially when you are uncomfortable in it—besides, you leave your body every night anyway, when you dream. On the other hand, really inhabiting your body, coming fully back to it, is a long process of learning. So the first priority is to land, to incarnate.

Yet we must also realize that there are other realities, and learn to be open to other spaces, even within this very body. We must incarnate and open ourselves, without discarnating; we must go beyond our form, yet not lose this form; we must go beyond ego, yet accept the fact that as long as we exist in this space-time, right up to our last breath, we have an ego. Yet it can be a more porous, transparent ego, a less painful one, more open, less closed, more free of this form and the elements, which compose it.

In my encounters with beings considered to be saints or bodhisatt-vas, I have been struck by the fact that they do have a well defined "me." In some lamas I have met, it is even a bit thick, with certain marked traits of character, ways of being, and so forth. But they are never ham-pered by these, or identified with them. Their "me" is open.

On the other hand, people I have met who consume great quantities of spiritual writings, and claim that there must be no ego, strike me as not very well incarnated, not really free in their actions and in their con-crete attitudes. In the Gospel of Thomas, it is said that whoever wants to become poor should first become rich. Then they can let go of these riches, for they will know that this is not true wealth. If you want to go beyond this "temporary identity" of yours, then begin by accepting it, and experiencing the relative happiness of a relative identity. Then you can truly see the illusion of it and open to ultimate Reality.

To be in the heart of form, and open to formlessness—this is also the great message of the Heart Sutra, or *Prajñaparamita:* "Form and form-lessness, finite and infinite, created and uncreated . . ." a moment comes when they are One, and we no longer oppose them to each other.

Even at the level of our own emotional experience, before we renounce all personal consolation from meditation and prayer, perhaps we would do best to first accept them. It was only after accepting such consolation that Thérèse of Lisieux, a great bodhisattva, was finally able to pray: "O Lord, I want no more consolations. I've had enough. Enough comforts, enough sweet syrup, and I return all comfort and consolation to you, for the well-being of all, for the salvation of all." This prayer became reality: the harsh asceticism and darkness of her last years are well known.

This reminds me of an event during my stay at the Grande Chartreuse monastery. The novitiate master told me: "You are too complacent in your consolations. We are not here to experience consolations. Here, we even refuse consolations." In those days, I was very obedient, so I began to pray for no consolations to be given to me. The only problem was, they began to greatly increase after that! Clearly, I was not yet ready for the "dark night of the soul," and the aridity of the inner desert!

There comes a day when we renounce consolation, and "spiritual experiences" and even more are given to us, but then comes another day when they are really taken away from us. The greatest happiness comes when we give up all personal happiness, wanting only to be happy for the good of all beings. This is the teaching of the Dalai Lama: "All sufferings, without exception, come from the desire for happiness for oneself, whereas perfect Buddha-hood is born of the desire to make others happy. This is why the bodhisattvas practice the total giving away of one's own happiness in exchange for that of others."

But in order to renounce one's own happiness, we must first taste this happiness, without clinging to it or trying to own it. In giving away one's own happiness for the well-being of others, we awaken to a different order of happiness. It is less "wet," more "dry," less dependent on sense-perception. It involves a more inward kind of perception, in the depths where a peace is to be found, which is perhaps far vaster than any we have known before.

The lives of saints offer plenty of examples, both in Buddhist and in Christian tradition. It is not my aim to offer such marvelous examples but to emphasize the work that must be done to realize this. I am more interested in offering tools than fruits. I would rather give you the right tool to cultivate your own garden than offer you a nourishing fruit from my own, which might nourish you but not for long.

My insistence on the importance of everyday practice is precisely so that you can taste the fruits of your own garden. Dreaming about fabulous and extreme examples such as Thérèse de Lisieux, is useless, and only makes us nostalgic, and even a little despairing, because their attainment seem so lofty in comparison to our own poor ability to love.

Rather than purchasing fruits, which temporarily satisfy our hunger, we can acquire tools and practices in the realms of sexuality, attachment, possessiveness, and repressed material. We can test our own doors, learn to open them, learn to give, and learn how to change our habits of speech for the better, as previously discussed.

As the proverb says: "Give a fish to a hungry man, and he will eat for a day. Teach him to fish, and he will eat for a lifetime." Our aim here is to construct a fishing pole. But that does not lead us to the river. It does no good to keep the pole in a closet at home! In other words, everything I am telling you must be tested and experienced by you in everyday life.

To realize compassion—the gift of oneself and the opening of the heart as a way of being—requires times of meditation, which are infinitely precious. They stimulate and renew the virtues of patience, discipline, and energy. The energy of meditation will lead you to the sixth perfection: transcendent wisdom, known as *prajñaparamita* in Sanskrit.

# TWENTY-FOUR

# WISDOM

This transcendent knowledge is a clear and direct experience of reality, the immediacy of mind in touch with reality. This has nothing to do with any sort of esotericism, nor with special states of consciousness. It is clarity of heart and mind. If our actions are not authentic, it is because we lack authentic vision of what is.

Meditation will prepare us for a more authentic way of seeing. When we come out of a true meditation, one that is not merely the experience of a special inner world, we are grounded more than ever in reality. This Reality traverses us, is within us, and yet is also infinitely more than we are. Through it, we see everything differently. The meditative mind sees disagreeable or agreeable things with equanimity, patience, and goodwill. Transcendent knowledge is seeing reality in utter simplicity.

The practice of the different exercises here will develop a quality of wisdom, of being grounded in what is. In this grounding and adaptability, true compassion can manifest.

Here is a Tibetan practice in which we can find inspiration in complete freedom:

"Think and meditate thus: I welcome all negativities, I fear none of them, I rejoice in them.

"Think this: I give away all my positive acts, all my past, present, and future happiness, all use of my physical abilities, and all my possessions, to all sentient beings. See every being as receiving these benefits, and nurture your own great joy at the thought that they really have received them.

"To make this transfer more vivid, imagine that with every in-breath, a dark-colored cloud, corresponding to all the harmful acts, sufferings, and concealments of other beings is breathed in through your nostrils into the deepest depths of your heart. Imagine that this act helps all beings to rid themselves forever of all their negativities and torments.

"Then, when you breathe out, imagine that all of your happiness, and all your virtues, pour out of your nostrils in the form of white light, penetrating all beings, and rejoice in the thought that this light helps them to have rapid access to awakening.

"Make a habit of this practice, directed by the in-breath and out-breath, and make it the central practice of your meditation.

"Even outside of moments of formal meditation, remember this practice, and do it.

"This is the very essence of spiritual initiation, as taught repeatedly by Shantideva: If I cannot exchange the totality of my well-being for the suffering of others, I will never realize awakening, and there will be no happiness in this cycle of existences."

I joyously welcome all negativity, all suffering, all refuse, like a black light, which I breathe in. I let it descend into my depths, and I breathe out the white light of prayers for happiness and peace toward all those who have made me suffer, or make me suffer. I wish them awakening, simplicity, and peace.

As Jesus says in the Gospel of Thomas, it is not what goes into a person that makes them impure but what comes out of them. This was in relation to questions about contamination from those who do not eat kosher food. He reminds us that it is not others who contaminate us but what comes out of our mouths in the form of harmful and negative words, which poison us and the world.

In the preceding Tibetan practice, we are assured that there is nothing to fear. This goes against the habitual mechanisms of ego. As long as we are caught in the mistrust, which is typical of ego, we are already contaminated, caught in dualism and fear.

Henceforth, our attitude is one of fearlessness, of welcoming everything, even the worst negativity, not keeping it but letting it pass through us. This bodhisattva practice is in remarkable harmony with the teaching of the Gospels. But it is not easy for us! We are so conditioned to see danger in the other, guilt in the other. Yet in this vision there is nothing that is dirty or dangerous to us. Everything depends on what comes out of us, on the way we look upon reality. Everything depends on the purity or impurity of our heart—whether or not light and love can radiate from us. The presupposition here is that we have been able to allow the transformation of suffering.

There is no morbidity whatsoever in this practice. There is no sadness in the injunction to rejoice, and to welcome the suffering of others. Some representations of Christ emphasize the dimension of suffering, and miss the dimension of the love that transforms suffering. We are not saved by Christ's suffering but by the love through which he transforms suffering! There are all too few representations of Jesus smiling upon the cross, yet there are some: the Christ of the Abbey of the island of Lérins, for example; and that of the monastery of Notre-Dame de Beaufort, in Brittany.

This recalls the Gospel of John: "My life cannot be taken from me, for I have already given it." This is the sovereign attitude of one who does not merely react to events. The Christ is not the "object" of events and suffering but the Subject of what happens to him.

**Question: If the Buddha is uninterested in happiness and even in awakening, as long as there are other beings in the world who suffer, does that not imply that he is doomed to perpetual despair, since there will always be unhappy and malevolent beings? Is the Buddha as sad as the Christ?**

When I hear your question, I also see images. Your question indicates that you harbor certain images of the Christ (like the one at Perpignan, for example), or like that representation of Christ, which caused Dostoyevsky to lose his faith. Your image is that of a dead Christ, a cadaver, as in the Basel museum, an image without hope, without the liberation of the passion, which Christ lived.

When we speak of suffering, of taking it upon oneself, you must beware of any suggestion of pain-worship, or any sort of masochism. When we welcome suffering, it does not mean that we consider it a good thing. We can welcome it because we no longer fear it, in order to transform it, to replace it with joy and peace. Within us is a love, which is capable of this.

Jean Guitton once told me of a quote by Louis-Marie Grignion de Montfort. Based on one of his own experiences, he declared that Christ on the cross is the apotheosis of joy. At the time this shocked me, and I found it unacceptable.

When one suffers not for oneself but for others, it is an entirely different kind of suffering, which is not separate from joy. This is paradoxical and difficult to explain in words. But we can perhaps find a clue in our own down-to-earth experience, when we recall certain moments in which we felt pain for someone we love. In such a moment, on some level, the love we felt was greater than the pain, and transformed it.

Our representations of Christ are inadequate, inasmuch as they do not show this, and focus only on the suffering. By contrast, most representations of the Buddha show a sublime smile. This causes some people to conclude that Buddhism is a religion of peace, serenity, and joy, whereas Christianity is a religion of pain, which cultivates suffering.

But true Christianity absolutely does not cultivate suffering! Christ healed and cared for the sick, he took upon himself the suffering of the world—not to harbor it but to liberate it through the alchemy of compassion.

Some of these images need to be changed.

There is enough suffering in the world, and it serves nothing to add our own to it. To desire the welfare of all living beings, to deliver them from their suffering, is to be deeply happy. This is where we must begin.

There is a legitimate need to be happy, but this happiness should not be a small, closed, selfish one. How real is happiness amidst the suffering of others? This is not true happiness at all—it is complacency and ignorance. How can you be happy when you know that others are suffering? This is the question you should ask.

But do not misunderstand me: I am not saying that renunciation of happiness itself is a service to humanity. If you are happy, then at least there is some place of true happiness in you, and this is a good place to start. But this place of happiness must grow—and it will become greater and truer, precisely to the extent that you are able to give it to others and make them a little happier.

If there is only one person on Earth whom you have made happier, then your life has not been lived in vain. Even the smallest acts of loving-kindness count, toward a dog, even toward a plant, whose flowering in spring you sense is a response to your care for it. I believe that our life is wasted if this gift within us is not somehow communicated. Even in extreme situations, where there is no human being to receive your love, offer it to all beings, offer it to life, offer it even to the wind! It will carry your love to the being who most needs it.

To welcome the world's suffering in oneself without rejection, fear, or misgiving requires great maturity, a great quality of heart. This is for children, or for the immature. Children need to receive and to be loved. This is work for true adults, and unfortunately they are rare. Many so-called adults are still caught in a childish attitude of demanding of life.

In this practice, our concern is no longer about what we receive, about having more, which never leads to true satisfaction. On the contrary, we must admit to ourselves that we have passed the age of demanding and neediness. Just as we have been weaned from our mother's breast, we must wean ourselves from sucking from others. Perhaps the moment has come when we can give from our hearts, from our deepest being? It has come! We can now start to give, and welcome those who may need us.

Again, this has nothing to do with morbidity or exaltation of pain, to "welcome suffering with joy," as it is said in the scriptures. When Mother Theresa was still able to work effectively with dying people, she did not have a sad face, nor did she whine about her hardships. She gave through her acts, and the greatest of these was her smile and her attention.

If you want to help a sick person, you must first heal yourself. Becoming sick along with them is of no help. I repeat: this path does not consist of suffering along with others. It consists of accepting their suffering and unhappiness into our own happiness, so as to transform it. Otherwise, one falls into a caricature, and a distortion of the image of Christ or of Buddha.

Why worship images of a Christ overwhelmed by pain? The real Christ welcomed his and others' pain with open arms and an open heart. This is the deeper symbolism of the cross: the total openness of a being who cares nothing for self-preservation, because he carries within him that fire, which can transform anything. He is the burning bush, crowned with thorns, whose flames, in Pentecostal terms, become "tongues of flame." He is the incarnation of a *coincidentia oppositorum*— a conjunction of opposites: suffering and joy.

The Buddha's smile is not that of someone who is indifferent, or in a blissful trance. It is the serene smile of one who knows both suffering and the transformation of suffering.

In the words of Charles de Foucauld:

I cannot help but be happy, knowing that God is God, that God is Love, that the ground of being is bliss and goodness. I know this from my own experience! . . . but at the same time, I cannot help but suffer, because I see that this Love is not recognized by others.

St. Francis is certainly one of the most joyous, spontaneous, and radiant of saints to be found in Christianity, yet also one grieved most deeply "because Love is not loved."

For me, this is what it means to be inhabited by compassion: someone who can no longer be despondent, nor unhappy, because they know that love is Love, that life is Life, and that Love and Life will have the last word, right in the heart of all our deaths. They live this experience, yet they also know that Love is not loved, that Life is not loved, and they perform their actions in order that there be a little less suffering.

If you wish to perform an action like this, begin from your happiness, and do not be unhappy because of the unhappiness of others. This is not easy to express in words, because we tend to interpret these texts far too psychologically. This naturally breeds fear, because we think, "Oh no, I'll lose my own little happiness—I've struggled so hard to be happy. What will be left of it if I open myself to the suffering of others?" The only answer is: "Observe! Test it, find out for yourself!" Yet people do exactly the opposite.

The more we cling to ourselves, the more we cling to our own happiness, the more it shrinks. We must have faith in life. Certainly it could take away this happiness to which we are so attached, but it will never take away that deeper happiness, which is the essence of joy and peace, because it is none other than our Being itself. Then we discover that our own little happiness expands into something far more grand, not only for ourselves but also for others.

Let us return to practice. The Tibetan practice I previously outlined is known as *Tonglen*. Literally, it means "exchanging." *Tong* means to give, and *len* means to receive, accept, welcome. The aim of this practice is to transform our inner attitude. It begins with everyday life: to see others with an attitude of goodwill, as if they were our hosts, rather than our enemies, or a threat to us. The enemy is the other, who does not think as we do, who does not love as we love, who always wants to harm us.

This openness, this gift, this welcoming, turns out to be the foundation of authentic love and compassion, in the willingness to exchange my happiness for the suffering of others. The first step is of course to be able to put oneself in another's place. In Gestalt psychology, this takes the form of an exercise where one sits for several minutes on a chair or cushion, and concentrates on imagining yourself as a person who inspires fear or worry in you, perhaps someone from your past, such as a mean uncle. Then you are asked to continue this exercise of imagining that you are that uncle, until you are able to see what led him to act in the way he did.

Putting yourself in another's place is an exercise of getting out of oneself, out of one's worldview, and seeing another as they see themselves. If you have problems with someone, simply take a moment to do this exercise. Begin by adopting their attitude, and their tone of voice— in a person's tone of voice, one can always read something about their feelings and emotions—this helps to understand them from the inside.

Tonglen begins by putting yourself in the place of others, and accepting them. This is the beginning of freeing ourselves from our own assumptions. On a psychological level, this will also enable us to begin to free ourselves of our aggressive tendencies, with a deeper understanding of others' motivations, and a larger, more intelligent understanding of any situation. The simple practice of putting ourselves in another's place is where compassion begins.

On a more radical level, exchanging our ego for another's and seeing how they see us, is a reversal of the fundamental habit of ego. Egocentrism literally means always putting oneself at the center of things. This reversal could be called *allocentrism,* where the other becomes the center.

It is also useful, for it gives us a greater, more realistic perception of an adversary's perspective. Then we are able to respond in a way, which is not limited by egocentrism. We are able to free ourselves of the need to always be in the right, to be the stronger or more beautiful one. This achieves an attitude, which no longer feeds conflict and the separation between self and other.

Little by little, one approaches nondualism, the experience of unity. This must be distinguished from undifferentiated consciousness, where distinctions are obliterated, and, which leads to psychotic states; inability to distinguish self from other is typical of many psychoses. This practice is very different from such a regressive state, and requires an ability to differentiate between self and other, yet not to be imprisoned in that self.

Further along on the bodhisattva path, we enter into the advanced spiritual practice of "exchange of merits." This is when we are able to say: "All merits I have acquired in this life, or in past lives, all the good I have done, I give to others."

This is often practiced when accompanying the dying, for their salvation and liberation. We offer the dying person all our good actions, our good karma, all the good energy we have accumulated. At this moment, there may occur something that is characterized as a transfer of consciousness, or a transfer of energy, so that the other receives all of our best-accumulated karma.

The essence of this practice is also found among Christian bodhisattvas, such as Thérèse of Lisieux, Teresa of Avila, and St. John of the Cross. A moment comes when they offer to others all the fruits of their prayers and ascetic practices. "Lord, this joy, which you have given me—give it to another." Their renunciation of this joy opens them to a higher and subtler joy. This is a paradox, which cannot be explained, only verified in one's own experience: the renunciation of joy for the benefit of others leads to even more joy. However, one must beware of clever tricks of the mind, which may scheme to renounce joy as a means of obtaining more joy! It won't work. This is the ego in action, and it is not easy to see through it.

This is why it is said, "The awakened say what they must, when they must, without knowing that they know." One could also say that bodhisattvas love when they must, and as they must but without any agenda, in a state of innocence.

Perhaps you know the parable of the Pharisee and the tax collector. Standing in front of the assembly at prayer, the Pharisee says "Me, me, me . . ." and the tax collector, standing behind him, says, "Come to my aid!" Many Christians who know this passage attempt to place themselves as far behind as possible, so as to demonstrate their humility! The ego is like a clever monkey, which can co-opt anything, even the most spiritual practices, so as to expand itself.

"Behold, how I suffer!" The pathology of it should be obvious. Yet many who speak like this consider themselves as mystics! The monkey-mind is constantly engaged in an internal monologue, such as: "I suffer, and live in suffering. I am righteous, unlike that rotten person, whom life has destined to make me suffer. I suffer because. . . . By the way, have you heard the latest news about what they're doing to the Kurds? How disgusting! And meanwhile, I suffer, because I am so generous . . ."

It is not your suffering that will help the situation in Kurdistan! It only adds suffering to suffering. There is already plenty of it in the world.

Even a simple, concrete, material gesture is better than this. At least it may have real consequences. Perhaps the first gesture is to experience a little more peace, a little more happiness, which is not selfishly enclosed. Again, this evokes the principle of the just attitude as one that adjusts itself . . .

The bodhisattva practice also renounces any experience of paradise, as long as others do not share it. In this, there is an awakening to a joy, peace, and happiness, which is unselfish. It is amazing to encounter such beings, especially when they are already living in considerable hardship themselves, and yet take on others' problems without being overwhelmed or in despair. It is clear that there is a force operating through them, which is beyond the human.

Consider contemporary examples, such as Abbé Pierre,* or Mother Theresa. Yet instead of putting them on a pedestal, we should simply recognize that they are able to really accomplish something to reduce suffering, in a nonemotional way.

Mother Theresa was not an emotional or sentimental individual. Yet the way she held babies showed a power of love that has nothing to

---

*[Abbé Pierre (1912–2007) was a French Catholic priest who was a member of the Resistance during WW II and founder of the Emmaus, an organization to help poor and homeless people and refugees. —*Ed.*]

do with emotionalism. She was free of the common emotional reaction of being horrified by suffering children. What good is such an attitude? We shed a tear, we feel more compassionate, but we have not reduced the suffering of the world. Even worse is when we add guilt to the mixture, poisoning our lives, and that of our families, because we are so much more fortunate than these suffering children.

We have all met people who confuse self-flagellation with the path of the bodhisattva. "What? You dare to enjoy a drink of whisky, when others are dying of thirst?" I have had the good fortune of meeting a number of persons that I consider to be bodhisattvas, and never once have I encountered such an attitude among them. Their response would be the opposite: "You need to drink whisky, my friend? Have a drink, and enjoy it! Then, perhaps you can better turn your attention to helping your neighbors. When you feel better, perhaps less tired and discouraged, don't shut down—you can go further, and do something worthwhile." This is also simple good sense. There is no problem with experiencing ordinary, mundane pleasures, and allowing them to be infused with spiritual energies.

To accept and receive happiness, yet not to close ourselves around it, to remain open and vulnerable to others' suffering, knowing that our happiness will never be complete as long as a single being is suffering— this is not an experience of sadness. It is an experience of liberation from the anguish of wanting to be happy at any price. This is the very moment when we become available for higher, more joyous energies.

This brings us to the heart of the teaching of loving our enemies. We learn to love what is unlovable, what is unpleasant. In spite of all the scholarly critiques of the Gospels, which cast doubt on whether certain words were really spoken by Jesus, or written by later redactors, we can be reasonably sure of this quote, at least: "Love your enemies."

This is a new evolutionary event. It is not natural to humans to love their enemies. Once when I was at Mount Athos, I asked a monk: "How can I be sure that I am in the presence of the Holy Spirit, that it is Christ living within me, instead of my ego telling spiritual tales?" He answered: "You can only be sure when you love your enemies! Ecstatic experiences, the totally amazing feeling of energy surging up your spinal column, or being immersed in radiant light, are not necessarily the Holy Spirit, however cosmic these energies may be. But when you love your enemies, you can be sure that the Christ is living within you."

It is so natural to love our friends—but our enemies? This is not at all something given by nature. It is only given by voluntary participation in a quality of being and love greater than ourselves.

When we confront suffering, we are of course taking something very negative into ourselves—not to cultivate it but to transform it. Suffering is not good, but it can become something good if we transmute it, using it as an opportunity to evolve.

We owe it to ourselves and to others to be happy. If your true desire is the welfare of others, and of humanity, then you will become happier, or at least less unhappy. To begin at the beginning: just a little less unhappy, a little less sad, less negative, less spiteful. Then, when we have become even a little happier, that small happiness will spread into the world. I do not believe that a really unhappy person can make others happy.

If we really desire the happiness of all beings, we must also accept happiness in ourselves, while knowing that it does not belong to us but to life itself, to the living One. The more fully we taste happiness, the greater the number of other beings we can share it with. Yet it can never be complete until it is shared by all.

Thus we can wish happiness for each other.

If you are a Buddhist, inspire yourself by thinking of the bodhisattvas. If you are a Christian, think of the Christ, who came not to be served by others but to serve them in joy, in peace, and in generosity. For these beings, these are not mere words, but acts, which go all the way, right up to their last breath. Even their death is a gift, and resurrection is born from this kind of death.

There is something vaster than death. Suffering, stupidity, and death will not have the last word . . .

Christ is resurrected!

# BETWEEN US: NOTHING

## THE UNITED STATES, OCTOBER, 1979

There were about twenty of us professors gathered around Huston Smith, waiting to welcome the Dalai Lama, who had been invited to our university, the only one he visited during his first trip to New York State.

After the customary speeches and ceremonies, we began to greet each other with impulsive joy. Suddenly, all titles, distinctions, and roles had vanished.

> *Between us: Nothing . . .*
> *Space*
> *for all beings, without exception.*
> *Even a rat had his own place to bathe in this clear*
>      *light.*
>
> *. . .*
>
> *I saw the world truly.*
> *His Holiness smiled at the computers.*
>
> *. . .*
>
> *Fear nothing*
> *otherwise, you mistake yourself for an object;*

*but do not fear that, either—*
*it's just a round stone*
*that wrinkles the river,*
*and does not stop its flow.*

*. . .*

*between us*
*may this Nothing abide*
*so that Meeting is always possible.*

# NOTES

## INTRODUCTION

1. OTU, Hameau de St-Hugon, 73110 Arvillard, France. Videocassette in French: *Sous l'arbre de la Bodhi* [Under the Bodhi Tree] the second Intertraditions pilgrimage.
2. Henri de Lubac, *La rencontre du bouddhisme et de l'Occident* [The Meeting of Buddhism and the West] (Paris: Aubier, 1952) citing Paul Claudel, *Connaissance de l'Est* [Consciousness of the East] (1907), along with the other quotations by J. B. du Halde, J. Grasset, P. Parennin, and Ch. le Gobien.
3. Henri de Lubac, ibid.
4. Romano Guardini, *The Lord* (Washington D.C.: Gateway Editions, 1982).

## CHAPTER 2. TRANSMISSION

1. Jean-Yves Leloup, *Ecrits sur l'hésychasm* [Writings on Hesychasm] (Paris: Albin Michel, 1990).

# INDEX